Globalization and Entrepreneurship

Globalization and Entrepreneurship explores the transformative impact of digital technologies on entrepreneurship across three distinct, but interconnected nations. It presents a comprehensive analysis of how digital advancements and AI are reshaping traditional business models and fostering economic growth in China, Japan, and Bangladesh. With its focus on emerging trends and practical case studies, this book offers a thorough exploration of digital entrepreneurship's role in driving innovation and addressing socio-economic challenges in these regions. Readers will benefit from a multi-dimensional view of globalization's effects on entrepreneurship, highlighting the unique contributions and interactions of China, Japan, and Bangladesh. The book examines the influence of digital transformation, AI, and globalization on business practices and economic development. It provides valuable insights into how different countries are adapting to and leveraging technological advancements for competitive advantage, offering actionable recommendations for policymakers, business leaders, and scholars interested in the future of global entrepreneurship. It is essential reading for academics, researchers, and practitioners in international business, digital entrepreneurship, and global economic studies. It is particularly useful for those interested in the strategic and practical implications of digital technologies in diverse economic contexts. Whether you are a scholar seeking to understand global entrepreneurial dynamics or a business leader aiming to navigate the complexities of international markets, this book offers critical insights into the evolving landscape of global entrepreneurship.

Mirjana Radović-Marković is a Professor and Principal Research Fellow at the University Business Academy, Novi Sad, Serbia and Hunan Normal University, Changsha, China.

Yao Ouyang is a Distinguished Professor in the School of Economics Shanghai University, China.

Md. Shajahan Kabir is a Professor in the Department of Rural Sociology at Bangladesh Agricultural University, Bangladesh.

Routledge Focus on Business and Management

The fields of business and management have grown exponentially as areas of research and education. This growth presents challenges for readers trying to keep up with the latest important insights. *Routledge Focus on Business and Management* presents small books on big topics and how they intersect with the world of business research.

Individually, each title in the series provides coverage of a key academic topic, whilst collectively, the series forms a comprehensive collection across the business disciplines.

Purpose-driven Innovation Leadership for Sustainable Development
A Qualitative Case Study Approach
Gaia Grant

Evolution of the Global Fitness Industry
Strategy, Sustainability and Innovation
Patrizia Gazzola, Enrica Pavione and Francesco Ferrazzano

Digital Transformation of Performing Arts
Trends in the Classical Music Industry
Salvino A. Salvaggio

Globalization and Entrepreneurship
Cases from China, Japan and Bangladesh
Mirjana Radović-Marković, Yao Ouyang and Md. Shajahan Kabir

For more information about this series, please visit: www.routledge.com/Routledge-Focus-on-Business-and-Management/book-series/FBM

Globalization and Entrepreneurship

Cases from China, Japan and Bangladesh

Mirjana Radović-Marković,
Yao Ouyang and
Md. Shajahan Kabir

Routledge
Taylor & Francis Group
NEW YORK AND LONDON

First published 2025
by Routledge
605 Third Avenue, New York, NY 10158

and by Routledge
4 Park Square, Milton Park, Abingdon, Oxon OX14 4RN

Routledge is an imprint of the Taylor & Francis Group, an informa business

ISBN: 978-1-032-98743-9 (hbk)
ISBN: 978-1-032-99111-5 (pbk)
ISBN: 978-1-003-60237-8 (ebk)

DOI: 10.4324/9781003602378

Typeset in Times New Roman
by Newgen Publishing UK

Contents

Figures

Pictures

Tables

Preface

Globalization is increasingly considered in the context of its impact on different countries and regions in the current turbulent times. Among many experts, the prevailing opinion is that globalization creates winners among large countries and that they benefit the most from it.

Our research on the global impact on entrepreneurship covers various aspects, including economic growth, innovation, job creation, and social development. It has been found that entrepreneurship can stimulate economic growth by creating new businesses and markets, leading to increased employment opportunities and technological development.

The countries that we analyzed in this research are China (second largest country), Bangladesh (eighth country on the list), and Japan (twelfth largest). Analyzing and comparing these three nations provides a multifaceted view of global dynamics, cultural richness, and economic interdependence. Each country contributes uniquely to the global mosaic, and understanding their interactions fosters a clearer view on our interconnected world. However, factors such as access to finance, the regulatory environment and cultural norms can influence the extent of entrepreneurship development in different countries. Therefore, this study looks at the impact of globalization on entrepreneurship in China and the other two selected countries, including their economic, social, and cultural specificities. The research outline has been specifically constructed to facilitate the design of interdisciplinary scientific research, and it allows for the combination of a range of methods. First of all, the authors concluded that the analysis of the quality of entrepreneurship through the global entrepreneurship index should indicate what actions are necessary to be undertaken in order to indicate the needs of entrepreneurs and the gaps in the entrepreneurial ecosystem.

The authors also noted that the effects of globalization are complex and can have both positive and negative consequences on various aspects of these countries, including their economies, cultures, and societies. In order to better perceive these differences and give a comparative analysis and the degree of their integration into the global economic world, different sources of literature were used in the analysis as well as our own research.

This book differs from other books because it presents the results of the analysis of the development path of China, Bangladesh, and Japan during the past decades and determines their participation in global flows at several different stages. In addition to the analysis of their role in the global economy in several stages of development, this study is particularly significant because of its focus on the future and the next phase of globalization.

Prof. Dr Mirjana Radović-Marković
Head of the project

PART I

A Framework for Conceptualizing the Impact of Globalization on Large Countries

1 Basic Concept and Different Dimensions of Globalization

Mirjana Radović-Marković

1.1 Introduction

1.1.1 Definition of a "Large Country"

The definition of a "large country" can vary depending on the context, and different criteria may be used to determine a country's size (Ouyang, 2022). Here are a few common ways to define large countries:

- *Land Area*: One of the most straightforward ways to define a large country is by its land area. In this context, countries like Russia, Canada, and China are considered large due to their vast landmass (World Population Review, 2024).
- *Population*: Another way to define a large country is by its population. Countries with a high population, such as China and India, are often considered large in terms of their demographic size. Namely, large country refers more to the country's population rather than its physical size (World Population Review, 2024).
- *Economic Power*: Some may define large countries by their economic strength, considering factors like GDP (Gross Domestic Product). In this sense, countries like the United States and China are often seen as large due to their economic influence (Grosse, Gamso, and Nelson, 2021).
- *Cultural or Geopolitical Influence*: Large countries can also be defined by their cultural or geopolitical influence on a global scale. For instance, the United States is often regarded as a large country in terms of its global cultural impact and political influence. Despite the U.S. remaining influential, the rapid development and rise of China means that it is competing for dominance (BBC, n.d.).

DOI: 10.4324/9781003602378-2

- *Geographic Diversity*: Countries with significant geographic diversity, such as varied landscapes and climates, can also be considered large in terms of their natural attributes. Brazil, for example, is known for its diverse geography (Rosenberg, 2019).

1.2 Impact of Globalization on Large Countries

Globalization is a complex and ongoing phenomenon that involves the increasing interconnectedness of countries and people across the world (Youmatter, 2019). It has had a profound impact on large countries in various ways. Here are some key points to consider:

- *Economic Integration*: Large countries often play a significant role in global trade and investment. They have the capacity to influence global markets, and globalization has enabled them to expand their economic reach through international trade agreements and multinational corporations. Large countries often outsource certain tasks or jobs to lower-wage countries, which can have both positive and negative economic effects. It can reduce costs for businesses but may lead to job displacement. Globalization also exposes large countries to currency fluctuations and economic crises in other parts of the world (International Trade Council, 2023). This can impact trade balances and economic stability.
- *Cultural Exchange*: Large countries with diverse populations can benefit from globalization through increased cultural exchange. Globalization has facilitated the spread of ideas, languages, and cultural practices, leading to greater cultural diversity within these countries.
- *Political Influence*: Large countries can wield considerable political influence on the global stage. They often participate in international organizations and negotiations, shaping global policies and agreements on issues like climate change, security, and human rights.
- *Challenges of Inequality*: Globalization can exacerbate economic and social inequalities within large countries. While some regions and groups benefit from increased economic opportunities, others may be left behind, leading to disparities in income, education, and access to resources. In addition, globalization can exacerbate income inequality within large countries. While some benefit from increased economic opportunities, others may suffer job losses or wage stagnation due to international competition.

- *Environmental Impact*: The environmental impact of large countries is magnified in a globalized world. Their resource consumption, pollution, and carbon emissions have far-reaching consequences for the planet, contributing to environmental challenges such as climate change. It is also important to point out that large countries may face increased pressure on natural resources due to globalization, which can have environmental and economic consequences.
- *Migration and Diversity*: Large countries may experience increased immigration and cultural diversity due to globalization. This can lead to social and political debates about immigration policies, multiculturalism, and integration.
- *Technological Advancements*: Large countries often lead in technological advancements. Their technological advancements drive globalization by enabling communication, transportation, and information exchange across borders. Globalization facilitates the flow of information and innovation, which can benefit these nations in terms of research, development, and competitiveness in emerging industries. Large countries invest heavily in research and development (WEF, 2021).

The map shows the ten largest countries in the world according to data from 2022 (Picture 1.1). India has taken over China, which until recently was the most populous country in the world.

The countries that we analyzed in this research are China (second largest country), Bangladesh (eighth country on the list), and Japan (twelfth largest). Analyzing and comparing these three nations provides a multifaceted view of global dynamics, cultural richness, and economic interdependence. Each country contributes uniquely to the global mosaic, and understanding their interactions fosters a clearer view on our interconnected world.

China has experienced significant economic globalization. It has become one of the world's largest economies and a major player in international trade. Its exports and imports have grown substantially over the years. It has attracted substantial foreign direct investment, especially in manufacturing and technology sectors. It has been a hub for multinational corporations seeking to tap into its large market and low-cost labor. In addition, China plays a pivotal role in global supply chains, particularly in manufacturing. It's often referred to as the "world's factory" due to its extensive production capabilities. China's cultural influence has also expanded globally, with its films, cuisine, and language gaining popularity in many parts of the world.

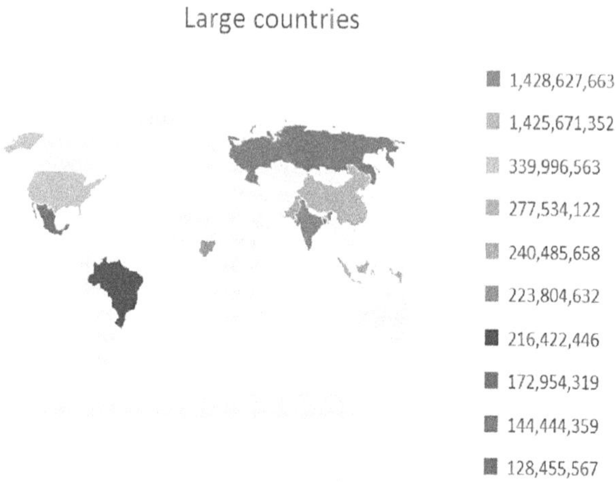

Picture 1.1 The Largest Countries in the World.

On the other side, Bangladesh has experienced globalization primarily through its garment industry. It's one of the world's largest apparel exporters, supplying clothing to many countries. A significant part of Bangladesh's globalization is through the remittances sent by Bangladeshi expatriates working abroad, which contributes to the country's economy. The information technology sector in Bangladesh has also grown, with the country providing services such as software development and outsourcing to global clients. Bangladesh receives substantial development aid from international organizations and foreign governments, which helps fund various projects and initiatives.

Japan has benefited from increased trade and foreign investment, contributing to its economic growth. It has become an important player in the global economy. Globalization has led to cultural exchange, with Japanese culture, including anime, cuisine, and fashion, gaining popularity worldwide. Japan is known for its technological innovations, and globalization has facilitated collaboration and knowledge sharing in fields like robotics, electronics, and automotive manufacturing.

Globalization has also posed challenges, such as competition from other economies and the need to adapt to changing global trade dynamics. Japan has faced demographic challenges, with an aging population and low birth rates. In line with this, globalization has influenced immigration and labor policies in response to these issues. Increased global trade has environmental consequences, affecting Japan's efforts to address climate change and resource consumption. We can conclude that globalization has brought both opportunities and challenges to Japan, shaping its economy, culture, and policies in various ways.

It is important to note that the effects of globalization are complex and can have both positive and negative consequences on various aspects of these countries, including their economies, cultures, and societies. In order to better perceive these differences and give a comparative analysis and the degree of their integration into the global economic world, different sources of literature were used in the analysis as well as our own research.

1.3 Theoretical Overview

Given the large number of theories related to the phenomenon of globalization, it is necessary to systematize them into theories originating from the views of classical scientists and those of contemporary thinkers. The difference between these two approaches is that classical scholars discussed cultural and sociological views, while modern scholars emphasized the economic and political aspects of the globalization phenomenon (Radović- Marković, and Tomaš, 2019). Namely, recent research on globalization might focus on its impact on income inequality, environmental sustainability, the effects of trade agreements, the rise of movement of people, and the role of technology in shaping global interactions.

1.3.1 The Most Important Theories about the Impact of Globalization on Large Countries

Bearing in mind that globalization has a great impact on large countries as well, through a review of the literature, we will deal with different theories that apply to this problem from different angles of consideration.

A selection of theories about impact of globalization on large economies s that are the most important according to our choice and that represent the basis of our research:

- *Economic Theory*: Globalization is often seen as a driver of economic growth and prosperity for large countries. One of the most influential economic theories of globalization is the neoclassical economic model (Asper and Kohl, 2015). This model presents the idea of convergence of prices and products all over the world, as a result of arbitrage and the clearing of markets. Another important economic theory is social liberalism (Hoerber and Anquetil, 2019) which emphasizes the importance of individual freedom and social justice.
- *Cultural Theory*: Globalization has facilitated the exchange of ideas, culture, and values across borders. This process has resulted in the standardization of cultural expressions globally, while also preserving cultural diversity and understanding (Crozet, 2017). The transmission of ideas, meanings, and values around the world in order to extend and intensify social relations is referred to as cultural globalization. This process is characterized by widespread consumption of cultures disseminated by the Internet, popular culture media, and international travel (Crozet, 2017). Some argue that this leads to cultural homogenization, where large countries may see a loss of their distinct cultural identities. Others see it as an opportunity for cultural diversity and the enrichment of society.
- *Political Theory*: The theory of state-centricism suggests that globalization challenges the authority of nation-states as international organizations and multinational corporations gain influence. Namely, political globalization refers to the intensification and expansion of political interrelations across the globe (Steger, 2020; Held and Maffettone, 2016). It raises political issues relating to state sovereignty and the question of whether the nation-state will survive globalization. Growing social, economic, and cultural interconnectedness has facilitated migration in large numbers and permeated borders. Contemporary globalization has put pressure on traditional forms of global governance by fostering the growth of supraterritorial social spaces and institutions that unsettle both familiar political arrangements and cultural traditions. The worldwide intensification of cultural interactions makes greater accommodation and tolerance possible, but it is just as likely to increase political resistance and opposition (Steger, 2020).
- *Environmental Theory*: Large countries often play a significant role in global environmental issues. According to a report by the Pew Research Center, climate change is considered the top global threat

across 19 countries (Pew Research Center, 2022). The report also reveals that a median value of 75% across 19 countries in North America, Europe, and the Asia-Pacific region label global climate change as a major threat.

Globalization can exacerbate environmental challenges, such as climate change and resource depletion, as large countries engage in extensive international trade and resource extraction. The relationship between large countries, globalization, and the environment is complex and multifaceted. While large countries have a significant impact on the environment, globalization has also led to increased awareness of environmental issues and the need for sustainable development. Many large countries are now taking steps to reduce their environmental impact and promote sustainable development.

- *Social Theory*: Globalization can impact the social fabric of large countries by changing patterns of migration, urbanization, and social inequality. According to a report by the Organisation for Economic Co-operation and Development (OECD), the growth of urban areas in large countries is often accompanied by increased social inequality (Burdett, 2016). This report also highlights that the distribution patterns of inequality vary significantly across the globe, with Africa and Asia set to experience exponential growth in the coming decades, thanks to increased birth rates and migration.
- *Technological Theory*: Globalization is closely tied to technological advancements. Large countries may benefit from access to global markets and innovation, but they also face challenges in protecting intellectual property and dealing with the digital divide. As per the International Monetary Fund (IMF), technological progress is a key driver of improvements in incomes and standards of living, and it is central to how global growth is generated and shared across countries (Aslam et al., 2018). They pointed out that China and Korea have started to make significant impact on the global fund of knowledge in recent years, joining the top five leaders in a number of sectors. In addition, large countries may benefit from technological advancements in several ways. For instance, they can leverage their economies of scale to produce goods more efficiently and with less manpower, which in turn makes those goods cheaper and allows businesses to scale faster (Drew, 2023). Additionally, globalization has accelerated the spread of technology across

borders by making it easier for countries to obtain access to foreign expertise (Aslam et al., 2018). However, it is important to note that technological advancements and globalization can also have negative consequences. For example, government and corporate surveillance of individuals and information processing relies largely on digital technologies and artificial intelligence, and therefore involves less human-to-human contact than ever before and more opportunities for biases to be embedded and codified in our technological systems in ways we may not even be able to identify or recognize (Wolff, 2021).

In conclusion, technological advancements and globalization are intertwined, and while they can bring about positive changes, they can also have negative consequences. It is important to strike a balance between the two and ensure that the benefits of technological advancements and globalization are distributed equitably.

- *Geopolitical Theory*: Globalization can influence the geopolitical landscape. Large countries may seek to expand their influence through globalization in several ways. For instance, they can leverage their economic power to negotiate favorable trade agreements with other countries, which can help to increase their exports and reduce their imports (Cevik, 2023). Additionally, large countries can use their economic clout to invest in other countries, which can help to create jobs and stimulate economic growth. However, it is important to note that globalization can also have negative consequences for smaller countries. For example, smaller countries may be forced to compete with larger countries on an uneven playing field, which can make it difficult for them to develop their own industries and compete in the global marketplace (Anderson, 1998).
- *Modernization Theory*: According to the theory, modernization refers to a model of a progressive transition from a "pre-modern" or "traditional" to a "modern" society. Proponents of modernization theory claim that modern states are wealthier and more powerful and that their citizens are freer to enjoy a higher standard of living. This theory suggests that as societies modernize and develop economically, they will inevitably become more interconnected and globalized (Bernstein, 1971; Munck, 2018). However, modernization theory is not without its critics. Critics argue that the theory is too simplistic and that it ignores the role of external factors.

- *Dependency Theory:* This theory argues that globalization can lead to a "core-periphery" relationship where developed countries dominate and exploit less developed ones, leading to economic and social imbalances. Namely, according to dependency theory, underdevelopment is mainly caused by the peripheral position of affected countries in the world economy. Typically, underdeveloped countries offer cheap labor and raw materials on the world market. These resources are sold to advanced economies, which have the means to transform them into finished goods. Underdeveloped countries end up purchasing the finished products at high prices, depleting the capital they might otherwise devote to upgrading their own productive capacity. Globalization can exacerbate the problems faced by underdeveloped countries by increasing their dependence on developed countries. For example, underdeveloped countries may be forced to compete with larger countries on an uneven playing field, which can make it difficult for them to develop their own industries and compete in the global marketplace. Additionally, globalization can lead to the exploitation of cheap labor and resources in underdeveloped countries, which can further perpetuate the cycle of underdevelopment (Parvati, 2022).
- *World Systems Theory*: Developed by Wallerstein (1993), this theory categorizes the world into core, semi-periphery, and periphery regions and explains how they interact economically and politically, leading to globalization dynamics. World-systems theory is a multidisciplinary approach to world history and social change that emphasizes the world-system (and not nation-states) as the primary unit of social analysis (Shaun, 2022).
- *Cultural Imperialism Theory*: This theory focuses on the influence of powerful cultures, often Western, on less powerful ones, leading to the spread of cultural values, media, and consumer products globally. Although Schiller (1969) is often identified as originating the theory, the conceptual basis for the theory has a shared history both within the United States as well as Latin American authors such as Mattelart (1976) and Schmucler (1975) theory among others. Namely, Schmucler was one of the Latin American authors who contributed to the theory of cultural imperialism. The theory describes the growing influence of the United States and its commercial media system around the world, specifically in the context of the Cold War, after the Second World War, when the United States and the Soviet Union were attempting to compel and persuade other countries to adopt their respective

socioeconomic systems. The theory specifically focused on the ways in which US culture was being spread to and sometimes imposed upon developing nations by US communications and media corporations.

- *Hyperglobalist Theory*: This theory sees globalization as a powerful force that erodes national sovereignty and creates a single, interconnected global society with minimal barriers to trade and communication. Hyperglobalists argue that globalization is a positive process characterized by economic growth, increasing prosperity, and the spread of democracy (Thompson, 2023). They believe that local cultures are being eroded primarily because of the expansion of international capitalism and the emergence of a homogeneous global culture. However, critics of hyperglobalism argue that the theory is overly optimistic and ignores the negative consequences of globalization, such as environmental degradation, social inequality, and the erosion of labor standards. They also argue that hyperglobalism underestimates the power of nation-states and the importance of local cultures and traditions (Thompson, 2023).
- *Skeptical Theory*: In contrast to hyperglobalism, this theory argues that globalization is not as all-encompassing as some believe and that nation-states and local cultures still play significant roles. Skeptics argue that globalization is a complex and multifaceted process that cannot be reduced to a single, unified phenomenon (Martell, 2007). They contend that globalization is not a new phenomenon, but rather a continuation of earlier forms of internationalization.
- *Transformationalist Theory*: This theory suggests that globalization is leading to fundamental changes in society, but the outcomes are unpredictable and depend on various factors, including policy choices and cultural dynamics. According to this theory, globalization is not a single, unified phenomenon, but rather a complex and multifaceted process that is transforming the world in a variety of ways (Mozaffari, 2001). Transformationalists believe that globalization is leading to the emergence of new forms of governance and regulation that challenge traditional forms of state sovereignty.

The abovementioned theories each offer different perspectives on the causes, consequences, and implications of globalization, and they continue to evolve as globalization itself changes and adapts over time.

1.4 Measuring Globalization Indicators: A Comparative Analysis for the Selected Countries

Measuring globalization is complex, and different indicators may yield different results. Researchers often use a combination of these methods to gain a comprehensive understanding of a country's level of globalization. Measuring the degree of globalization of a country involves assessing various economic, social, and political factors. Here are some common indicators and methods used to measure a country's level of globalization:

1.4.1 Economic Indicators

- *Trade Openness*: This measure is used to assess the degree of a country's integration into the global economy. A higher value of trade openness indicates that a country is more involved in international trade, while a lower value indicates the opposite. According to the World Bank, the trade openness of a country is defined as the sum of its exports and imports as a percentage of its GDP. Here are the trade openness values for China, Japan, and Bangladesh (Table 1.1):

The data is based on the latest available information from the World Bank (TheGlobalEconomy.com, 2020).

China has inked 19 free-trade agreements involving 26 countries and regions, and free-trade agreements have brought closer ties between China and its trade partners. Japan is the third largest economy in the world after the United States and China, and it is the fourth largest importer of U.S. products after Canada, Mexico, and China (OECD, 2022). Bangladesh has been actively promoting and strengthening economic cooperation with nations in the Asia-Pacific region (OECD, 2011).

Table 1.1 Trade Openness

Country	*Trade Openness*
China	37.5%
Japan	36.6%
Bangladesh	32.5%

Source: Author prepared according to data of The Global Economy (2020b).

- *Foreign Direct Investment (FDI)*: Foreign Direct Investment (FDI) is an investment made by a company or individual in one country into business interests located in another country. It is a long-term investment and is considered to be more stable than other forms of investment. FDI can be in the form of mergers and acquisitions, building new facilities, reinvesting profits earned from overseas operations, and intra-company loans. Assess the inflow and outflow of foreign investments. According to the UNCTAD's World Investment Report 2023, foreign direct investment (FDI) in Bangladesh increased by 12.9% to $2.9 billion in 2021, compared to $2.56 billion in 2020. The total stock of FDI was estimated at $21.58 billion in 2022 (Table 1.2). Table 1.2 also shows that greenfield investments are significantly reduced (–87%) in Bangladesh in 2022. This decline is driven by weak investment interest in garment manufacturing, one of the country's main export industries. However, the export-oriented clothing industry is still a significant recipient of FDI, with major investors from the Republic of Korea, Hong Kong, and China. The Bangladesh Central Bank's data show that the textile sector was the biggest gross FDI recipient, netting $1.166 billion in 2021, with an annual growth of around 81% (UNCTAD, 2023).

A report produced by UNCTAD (2023) showed that the Bangladesh government is actively seeking to attract foreign investment, particularly in the areas of energy and infrastructure.

China has been the second largest recipient of foreign direct investments (FDI) worldwide, attracting approximately $181 billion in 2021. In China, FDI inflows were $144.4 billion in 2020, a 4% increase from 2019. However, foreign direct investment (FDI) into China declined by 9.4% year-on-year to CNY 987.01 billion in the first

Table 1.2 Foreign Direct Investment (FDI) in Bangladesh

Foreign Direct Investment	*2020*	*2021*	*2022*
FDI Inward Flow (million USD)	2,564	2,896	3,481
FDI Stock (million USD)	19,395	21,582	21,158
Number of Greenfield Investments	16	15	21
Value of Greenfield Investments	805	1,036	456

Source: Author prepared according to UNCTAD (2023).

ten months of 2023. Direct investments in the service sector decreased by 15.9%, while they increased in the production sector by 1.9%. At the same time, investments in high-tech production increased significantly by 9.5%, with the medical equipment and instrument manufacturing industry achieving a growth rate of 34.6%, and the electronic and communication equipment manufacturing industry growing by 14.8%. In addition, investments in the construction industry and research and development and design services increased by 30.0% and 15.9%, respectively.

Analyzing the UNCTAD's 2022 World Investment Report, it is noted that Japan's FDI declined by 30% to $10.70 billion in 2020, reflecting a 25% decline in FDI from MNEs in the United States. It reached $24.65 billion in 2021. Japan's FDI stock was estimated at about $232.31 billion in 2021 and $256.93 billion in 2021. During the same year, Japan's foreign direct investment (FDI) flows to China amounted to almost $10.2 billion (UNCTAD, 2023).

Finally, it can be concluded that according to the World Investment Report 2023 by UNCTAD, global foreign direct investment (FDI) fell by 12% in 2022, and the report predicts that the global FDI flows will continue to fall in 2023 due to the ongoing geopolitical and economic risks (UNCTAD, 2023).

1.4.2 Gini Coefficient

The Gini coefficient is a statistical measure that is used to represent unequal distributions of income, e.g. income distribution. It can take any value between 1 and 100 points (or 0 and 1). The closer the value is to 100, the greater is the inequality. In other words, a high Gini coefficient reflects a large gap between a country's richest and poorest citizens.

The warning level set by the United Nations is 40 or 0.4. It is important to note that different sources may use different data collection and survey methods, which can lead to variations in the reported Gini coefficient values.

China's Gini coefficient is higher than the global average of 38 (World Population Review, 2023a). According to Statista (2023), the Gini coefficient for China in 2022 was 46.7%. On the other hand, IndexMundi reports that the Gini index (World Bank estimate) in China was 38.20% as of 2019. The reason for such a high Gini coefficient in China is found in the income gap between urban and rural areas. In our opinion, it is a major contributor to income inequality. In addition, the regional differences play a significant role in income inequality in China. Namely, variations across Chinese provinces account for about 12% of the country's overall income inequality (Wu, 2015).

Statistical data showed that the Gini index for Japan was 37.9 in 2022 (World Bank, 2023). On the other hand, the Gini coefficient for Japan according to the World Population Review was 33.0 in 2022. In Japan, the aging population and the decline in the number of young people entering the workforce have also contributed to income inequality.

According to the World Bank, the Gini coefficient of Bangladesh was 31.8% in 2022 (CEIC Data, 2021), which is a decrease from the previous figure of 32.4% for December 2016. This indicates a moderate level of income inequality in the country. It's important to note that income inequality in Bangladesh has been deepening over the past few years.

The Gini Coefficient related to income rose to 0.499 in 2022 from 0.482 in 2016. As per the latest data, 10% of the population in Bangladesh holds 44% of the total national income (The Daily Star, 2024).

Numerous measures are applied to reduce inequality, such as encouraging education, as well as labor protections such as collective bargaining, workplace safety regulations, and anti-discrimination laws. These measures can help reduce income inequality by ensuring that workers are treated fairly and have access to good-paying jobs.

1.4.3 Financial Integration

- *Capital Flows*: Based on statistical data, China had a capital and financial account deficit of $626 hundred million in the third quarter of 2023. In the period from 1998 to 2023, capital flows in China averaged –$289.10 hundred million, reaching a record high of $759.97 hundred million in Q1 2018 and a record low of –$1411.15 hundred million in Q3 2022 (State Administration of Foreign Exchange, China, 2023). Bangladesh's capital flows have been relatively stable, with a net inflow of $1.5 billion in 2020.

Capital flows in emerging Asia are influenced by a combination of factors, including global liquidity conditions, monetary policies in advanced economies, and domestic macroeconomic and financial conditions (CEPR, 2011).

- *Currency Exchange Rates*: Currency exchange rates are subject to fluctuations due to various factors such as economic policies, geopolitical events, and market sentiments. The stability of exchange rates is a crucial factor in international trade and investment. The convertibility of a currency refers to the ease with which it can be exchanged for another currency. A currency with high convertibility can be easily traded on forex markets with little to no restrictions.

The European Central Bank (ECB) recently published its annual review of the international role of the euro. According to the report, the international role of the euro remained stable in 2021, with its share across various indicators of international currency use averaging around 19% (ECB, 2022).

The Yuan has been one of the world's most stable major currencies, with daily fluctuations of up to 2% from its reference rate against the dollar (The Economist, 2020). Although it has never hit that limit, China has grown comfortable with allowing bigger swings within it, which may have contributed to its stability.

1.4.4 Cultural and Social Indicators

- *Migration*: According to the World Migration Report 2022 by the International Organization for Migration, more than 281 million people were living in countries other than their countries of birth in 2020, which equates to 3.6% of the global population (UN MIGRATION, 2022). The report also states that more than 40% of all international migrants worldwide in 2020 (115 million) were born in Asia, nearly 20% primarily originating from six Asian countries including India (the largest country of origin), China, Bangladesh, Pakistan, Philippines, and Afghanistan (UN MIGRATION, 2022).

    1. In China, the borders remain tightly controlled as of 2022. However, the country has been experiencing a significant increase in the number of immigrants in recent years. According to the World Migration Report 2020, more than

115 million international migrants worldwide in 2020 were born in Asia, with China being one of the top countries of origin (Speelman, 2022).

2. In Japan, the number of foreign residents has been increasing in recent years. According to Nayyar (2002), the country has been importing temporary workers due a labor scarcity.
3. In Bangladesh, the movement of people across borders is a significant issue. The recruitment processes and employment abroad can easily devolve into a human rights issue, especially for lower-skilled migrant workers (Hajro et al., 2022)

- *Cultural Exchanges*: In China, the government has been actively promoting Chinese culture and language through various initiatives (Chen, 2009). The country has been investing in the establishment of Confucius Institutes around the world, which are non-profit public institutions that aim to promote Chinese language and culture (Xu, Zhang, 2017; Jun, 2021). Additionally, the Chinese government has been investing in the film industry, with the aim of promoting Chinese culture and values to a global audience (Wiest, 2016). On the other hand, anime and manga have been popular Japanese cultural exports for decades. The popularity of these forms of entertainment has led to the establishment of anime and manga conventions around the world, where fans can gather and celebrate their love for Japanese pop culture (UNESCO, n.d.). Furthermore, the Japanese government has been promoting Japanese culture through the establishment of the Japan Foundation, which aims to promote cultural exchange between Japan and other countries. In addition, in Bangladesh, the government has been promoting the country's cultural heritage through various initiatives. For example, the government has been organizing the Dhaka International Film Festival, which showcases films from Bangladesh and other countries (UNESCO, n.d.). Further, the country has been investing in the establishment of cultural centers around the world, which aim to promote Bangladeshi culture and heritage.

1.4.5 Political and Institutional Factors

- **Membership in International Organizations**: The analyzed countries are members of numerous global organizations such as the United Nations, the World Trade Organization, etc. We will list some of the most important ones with regard to the membership of China, Japan, and Bangladesh in international organizations:

1. **China**: China is a member of several international organizations, including the United Nations (UN), World Trade Organization (WTO), World Customs Organization (WCO), and the International Monetary Fund (IMF) (intrepidsourcing.com, n.d.). China's participation in these organizations has been increasing in recent years, and it has been actively seeking to strengthen its position within the system of international institutions.
2. **Japan**: Japan is also a member of several international organizations, including the UN, WTO, Asian Development Bank, and the Colombo Plan. Japan has been involved in world-wide economic groupings largely made up of, or dominated by, the industrialized countries of Western Europe and North America (Japan and the United Nations, n.d.).
3. **Bangladesh**: Bangladesh is the largest contributing country to UN peacekeeping operations. It is also a member of several international organizations, including the UN, ASEAN Regional Forum, IMF, World Bank, and WTO. Bangladesh also participates in regional integration in the Indo-Pacific region through organizations such as the Bay of Bengal Initiative for Multi-Sectoral Technical and Economic Cooperation (BIMSTEC), Bangladesh-Bhutan-India-Nepal (BBIN) Initiative, the South Asian Association for Regional Cooperation (SAARC), and the Indian Ocean Rim Association (IORA) (US Department of State, 2022).

Membership in international organizations can have a significant impact on a country's foreign policy and global influence. By participating in these organizations, countries can work together to address global challenges and promote international cooperation.

- *Political Stability*: Political stability is a crucial factor in determining the ease of doing business in a country. A stable political environment provides a predictable business landscape, enabling organizations to plan and invest with confidence. Conversely, political instability, marked by frequent changes in leadership or social unrest, can disrupt business operations, supply chains, and consumer behavior (MBA Skool Team, n.d.).

Here's a brief overview of the political environment and ease of doing business in China, Japan, and Bangladesh:

1. **China**: China has a one-party system, with the Communist Party of China (CPC) being the only legal political entity. The country has a centralized political structure, with the CPC holding significant control over the economy. Despite this, China has been successful in attracting foreign investment and has a favorable business environment. According to the World Bank's Ease of Doing Business Index, China ranks 31st out of 190 countries (Doshi, Kelley, and Simmons, 2019).
2. **Japan**: Japan is a parliamentary representative democratic constitutional monarchy, with the Emperor of Japan serving as the ceremonial head of state. The country has a stable political environment and a highly developed economy. Japan ranks 29th in the Ease of Doing Business Index (Doshi, Kelley, and Simmons, 2019).
3. **Bangladesh**: Bangladesh is a parliamentary democracy, with the President of Bangladesh serving as the head of state. The country has a mixed economy and has made significant progress in recent years in improving its business environment. Bangladesh ranks 168th in the Ease of Doing Business Index.

1.4.6 Technology and Communication

- *Internet and Mobile Connectivity*: According to the Speedtest Global Index, last year 2022 saw great progress in mobile internet speeds, which became almost 17% faster from November 2021 to November 2022. At the same time, fixed broadband speeds also increased for 28%. These improvements are a testament to the ongoing efforts to improve internet infrastructure and connectivity around the world (Fomon, 2023).

According to a report from Statista, the Asia-Pacific region has the highest number of internet users in the world, with the biggest shares of internet users in East Asia and Oceania (Leander von Kameke, 2023). The same report states that South Asia has the lowest number of internet users in the region. China is one of the world leaders in terms of smartphone user base and mobile connectivity. As of June 2022, about 1.05 billion people had subscribed to mobile internet

Table 1.3 Top 10 Countries with the Fastest Mobile Internet Speeds (Mbps), 2021

1.	UAR	238.6
2.	South Korea	202.61
3.	Norway	177.72
4.	Qatar	182.18
5.	**China**	**165.38**
6.	Kuwait	157.18
7.	Saudi Arabia	155.97
8.	Cyprus	144.64
9.	Bulgaria	142.27
10.	Switzerland	135.7

Source: Author prepared according to World Population Review, (2023a).

services in the country, equivalent to 73% of its population (Lai Lin Thomala, 2023). According to the latest available data (Statista, 2023), over 350 Chinese cities have 5G availability, making it the best ranked country in the world. By 2025, the 5G network is expected to account for 47% of total connections with 1.28 billion users in China, while the number of 5G users by 2030 is expected to reach 1.6 billion (Tomás, 2023).

A report conducted by the World Population Review has shown that China ranks fifth in the world in terms of mobile internet speeds, with an average speed of 165.38 Mbps (World Population Review, 2023b).

Table 1.3 shows that China is ranked fifth among the ten countries with the fastest mobile internet in the world. The first position is held by the United Arab Emirates. China jumped four places from sixth to second for fixed broadband Internet, improving its median download speed from 146.62 Mbps in 2021 to 214.58 Mbps in 2022 (Fomon, 2023).

According to the Speedtest Global Index, Japan was ranked 58th in the world for mobile speeds and 24th for fixed broadband speeds during August 2023 (Speedtest, 2023).

In Bangladesh, the average mobile internet speed is 18.58 Mbps (Rank 111) (Bangladesh Median Country Speeds, 2023). The Speedtest Global Index shows that Bangladesh ranked 104th in the world for fixed broadband speeds during August 2023 (Taylor, 2023). The World Bank reports that there were about 11.1 million fixed broadband subscriptions registered in Bangladesh in 2021, an increase of over a million on the previous year (Taylor, 2023).

- *Information Flow* refers to the movement of information from one place to another, often within an organization or system. It involves the transfer of data between different entities, such as people, departments, or systems, ensuring that the right information reaches the right people at the right time. Below are the flows of information for each country considered:
  1. **China**: China has a notoriously strict media environment, with the government relying on censorship to control information in the news, online, and on social media. The government uses libel laws, criminal charges, and other means to punish journalists who report on sensitive topics, and foreign journalists are often harassed and expelled. According to a report by the Foreign Correspondents' Club of China, press freedom in China has been rapidly deteriorating, with correspondents often only learning of press events after they occur (DW, 2022).
  2. **Japan**: Japan is generally considered to have a free and open media environment, with a strong tradition of investigative journalism and a high degree of press freedom. However, there are concerns that the government is becoming more aggressive in its efforts to control the media, particularly in the wake of the Fukushima nuclear disaster (Cheshmehzangi, 2021).
  3. **Bangladesh**: Bangladesh has a mixed record on press freedom, with journalists facing harassment, intimidation, and violence from both state and non-state actors. The government has been accused of using repressive laws to silence critical voices, and journalists have been arrested and prosecuted for their reporting. However, there are also independent media outlets that are able to operate freely and report on sensitive issues (Lemberg, 2021).

1.4.7 Environmental Indicators

- **Carbon Emissions**: Carbon emissions are a significant contributor to global environmental issues. According to Our World in Data, Bangladesh had a carbon dioxide (CO_2) emissions per capita of 0.4 metric tons in 2019, which is lower than the global average of 4.8 metric tons per capita (Ritchie and Roser, 2022a). China, on the other hand, had a CO_2 emissions per capita of 7.5 metric tons in

2019, which is higher than the global average. Ritchie and Roser (2022b) pointed out that Japan had a CO_2 emissions per capita of 7.9 metric tons in 2019, which is also higher than the global average. According to Our World in Data, Japan's carbon dioxide emissions in 2019 were 1.2 billion metric tons (Ritchie and Roser, 2022b) and China's carbon dioxide emissions in 2019 were 10.2 billion metric tons (BBC, 2021). However, China has pledged to reach net-zero emissions by 2060 with a peak no later than 2030. Japan, on the other hand, has set a target of reducing its greenhouse gas emissions by 46% by 2030 (Ritchie and Roser, 2022b).

The main sources of carbon dioxide emissions in China are coal and oil (Blokhin, 2023). In Japan, the primary sources of carbon dioxide emissions are electricity and heat production (Ritchie and Roser, 2022b).

It is important to note that carbon emissions are not the only factor contributing to global environmental issues. Other factors such as deforestation, pollution, and waste management also play a significant role.

- *Global Supply Chains*: We will take into account the example of China, Bangladesh and Japan and compare their influence in this domain. In this context, China is a major player in the global supply chain, with a skilled labor force, extensive supplier ecosystem, and fast-growing domestic markets. As a result, complex, tightly integrated supply networks now link China with the rest of the world (McKinsey, 2023). Japan is also a significant player in the global supply chain, with a highly developed manufacturing industry and a reputation for producing high-quality goods. Japan is a major exporter of automobiles, electronics, and machinery, and is home to many of the world's largest automakers (NSW Treasury, 2022). Further, Bangladesh is a major player in the global textile and garment industry, with a large and growing workforce and a reputation for producing high-quality products at low cost. The country is the world's second-largest exporter of ready-made garments, after China.
- *Globalization Indexes*: Several organizations produce globalization indexes, such as the KOF Globalization Index, which combine multiple indicators to provide a comprehensive ranking. This index measures the economic, social, and political dimensions of

globalization and provides a comprehensive ranking. The index is measured on a scale of 1 to 100 and distinguishes between de facto globalization and de jure globalization in the overall index and in the economic, social, and political components. According to the latest data, KOF index in China was 46 in 2020. At the same time, Japan had a score of 75, while Bangladesh had a score of 50 (The Global Economy.com, 2020a).

- *Qualitative Data*: Surveys and expert opinions can also be valuable in understanding a country's globalization, especially in assessing the cultural and political dimensions. In this context, Hofstede (1991) a European research consultant, provided a framework for understanding cultural differences; important dimensions of national character have been identified in his six-dimension model. The Hofstede model, or the 6-D Model of National Culture, is a way of understanding the culture of a country based on its cultural values. The model has been used to help organizations improve communication and cooperation between people from different cultures. This model is a useful framework for understanding how cultural differences can make an impact on business dealings. Minkov and Kaasa (2022) have revised the Minkov-Hofstede model of culture.

1.5 Conclusion

The impact of globalization on small and large countries can differ, with both opportunities and challenges. Globalization is a complex phenomenon that has far-reaching implications for societies, economies, cultures, and politics around the world. Different theories of globalization provide different perspectives on the causes, consequences, and dynamics of globalization. Analyzing different theories of globalization is important because it helps us understand the complex and multifaceted nature of globalization and its implications for different aspects of our lives. In addition, considering these theories can help us gain more understanding of the ways in which globalization affects different countries and regions, including large countries.

Investigating the impact of globalization on China, Japan, and Bangladesh is important for several reasons, such as the following:

- ➢ Firstly, China is one of the world's largest economies and has been a major beneficiary of globalization. The impact of globalization on

China has been profound, with globalization helping China achieve rapid economic growth and poverty reduction (Grosse, Gamso, and Nelson, 2021). Investigating the impact of globalization on China can help us better understand the opportunities and challenges that come with globalization.

- Secondly, Japan is another major economy that has been impacted by globalization. The globalization of the Japanese economy has led to increased competition and the need for Japanese companies to adapt to changing market conditions (Urata, 2022). Investigating the impact of globalization on Japan can help us better understand how globalization is affecting the Japanese economy and society.
- Finally, Bangladesh is a developing country that has been impacted by globalization in a number of ways. Globalization has led to increased economic activity in Bangladesh, with the country becoming a major exporter of garments and textiles. However, globalization has also led to increased inequality and environmental degradation in Bangladesh (Grosse, Gamso, and Nelson, 2021). Investigating the impact of globalization on Bangladesh can help us better understand the opportunities and challenges that come with globalization for developing countries.

In conclusion, while globalization can provide opportunities for large countries to expand their influence, it is important to ensure that the benefits of globalization are distributed equitably and that smaller countries are not left behind.

References

Anderson, E.W. (1998). The Effects of Globalization on Geopolitical Perspectives. *GeoJournal*, Vol. 45, No. 1/2, pp. 105–108. www.jstor.org/stable/41147225.

Aslam, A., Eugster, J., Ho, G., Jaumotte, F., and Piazza, R. (2018). Globalization Helps Spread Knowledge and Technology Across Borders. Available at: Globalization Helps Spread Knowledge and Technology Across Borders [accessed January 12, 2024].

Asper, P., and Kohl, S. (2015). *Economic Theories of Globalization. The Routledge International Handbook of Globalization Studies*. New York & London: Routledge. Available at: Economic theories of globalization | 4 | v2 | The Routledge International [accessed January 12, 2024].

Bangladesh Median Country Speeds (October 2023). Available at: www.speedtest.net/global-index/bangladesh [accessed January 10, 2024].

BBC (2021). Report: China Emissions Exceed All Developed Nations Combined. BBC News. Available at: Report: China emissions exceed all developed nations combined [accessed January 12, 2024].

BBC (n.d). The USA's International Influence – The USA's involvement in international organisations . BBC Bitesize. Available at: The USA's involvement in international organisations - The USA's international influence - Higher Modern Studies Revision - BBC Bitesize [accessed January 10, 2024].

Bernstein, H. (1971). Modernization Theory and the Sociological Study of Development. *Journal of Development Studies*, Vol. 7, No. 2, pp. 141–160.

Blokhin, A. (2023). The 5 Countries That Produce the Most Carbon Dioxide (CO2). Available at: The 5 Countries That Produce the Most Carbon Dioxide (CO2) (investopedia.com) [accessed January 11, 2024].

Burdett, R. (2016). *Inequality and Urban Growth.* OECD. Available at: Inequality and urban growth | OECD [accessed January 10, 2024].

CEIC Data (2021). Bangladesh BD: Gini Coefficient (GINI Index): World Bank Estimate. Available at: Bangladesh BD: Gini Coefficient (GINI Index): World Bank Estimate | Economic Indicators | CEIC [accessed January 10, 2024].

Cevik, S. (2023). Long Live Globalization: Geopolitical Shocks and International Trade. Available at: Long Live Globalization: Geopolitical Shocks and International Trade [accessed February 12, 2024].

Chen, S.X. (2009). Explaining Individuating Behavior Across Cultures: The Contributions of Values and Social Axioms. In: K. Leung and M.H. Bond (Eds.), *Psychological Aspects of Social Axioms: Understanding Global Belief Systems*. New York: Springer SBM, pp. 293–315.

Cheshmehzangi, A. (2021). From Transitions to Transformation: A Brief Review of the Potential Impacts of Covid-19 on Boosting Digitization, Digitalization, and Systems Thinking in the Built Environment. *Journal of Building Construction and Planning Research*, Vol. 9, pp. 26–39. https://doi.org/10.4236/jbcpr.2021.91003

Crozet, C. (2017). *Globalization and Culture*. Berlin: Springer.

Doshi, R., Kelley, J., and Simmons, B. (2019). The Power of Ranking: The Ease of Doing Business Indicator and Global Regulatory Behavior. Available at: doshikelleysimmons_edb_penultimate.pdf [accessed February 10, 2024].

Drew, C. (2023). Technological Globalization – Examples, Pros and Cons. Available at: Economic Globalization – Pros and Cons (with Examples) [accessed February 11, 2024].

DW (2022). Press Freedom Rapidly Deteriorating In China – Report. Available at: Press freedom rapidly deteriorating in China — report – DW – 01/31/2022 [accessed December 10, 2023].

ECB (2022). International Use of the Euro Remained Stable in 2021. Available at: International use of the euro remained stable in 2021 [accessed December 10 2023].

Fomon, J. (2023). The Speedtest Global Index Shows These Countries Sped Forward for Internet Experience in 2022. Available at: The Speedtest Global Index Shows These Countries Sped Forward for Internet Experience in 2022 | Ookla® [accessed December 13, 2023].

Grosse, R., Gamso, J., and Nelson, R.C. (2021). China's Rise, World Order, and the Implications for International Business. *Management International Review*, Vol. 61, pp. 1–26. https://doi.org/10.1007/s11575-020-00433-8

Hajro, A., Žilinskaitė, M., Gibson, C., et al. (2023). *Movement of People across Borders: Transdisciplinary Research to Meet the Challenges in Migration, Business, and Society - CBS Research Portal*. Academy of Management Discoveries Vol 9. No. 2, pp 125-131. ISSN 2168-1007

Held, D., and Maffettone, P. (2016). Globalization and Global Political Theory, *Global Policy Journal*. Available at: Globalization and Global Political Theory | Global Policy Journal [accessed December 10, 2023].

Hoerber, T., and Anquetil, A. (2019). *Economic Theory and Globalization*. Berlin: Springer.

Hofstede, G. (1991). *Cultures and Organizations: Software of the Mind: Intercultural Cooperation and Its Importance for Survival*. New York: McGraw-Hill.

International Trade Council (2023). Understanding the Impact of Currency Fluctuation on Global Trade. Available at: Understanding-the-Impact-of-Currency-Fluctuation-on-Global-Trade.pdf [accessed December 10, 2023].

intrepidsourcing.com (n.d.). Trade Associations: China's Membership in WTO and Co. Available at: China's Trade Organizations: WTO & WCO Associations.

Japan and the United Nations (n.d.). 000075164.pdf. Available at: Japan and the United Nations – Wikipedia [accessed December 14, 2023].

Jun, X. (2021). Three steps for Chinese culture to 'go global'. Chinese Social Sciences Today. Facts and Figures 2023 - Subscriptions. Available at: CSSN-Three steps for Chinese culture to 'go global' [accessed December 10, 2023].

Lai Lin Thomala (2023). Mobile Cellular Subscriptions (Per 100 People). Available at: Mobile cellular subscriptions (per 100 people) | Data (worldbank.org) [accessed November 12, 2023].

Lemberg, D. (2021). *Barriers Down: How American Power and Free-Flow Policies Shaped Global Media*. New York: Columbia University Press.

Martell, L. (2007). The Third Wave in Globalization Theory. *International Studies Review*, Vol. 9, No. 2 (Summer 2007), pp. 173–196.

Mattelart, A. (1976). Cultural Imperialism in the Multinationals' Age. *Instant Research on Peace and Violence*, Vol. 6, No. 4, 160–174.

MBA Skool Team (n.d.). *Political Environment – Definition, Importance, Factors & Example*. Available at: www.mbaskool.com/business-concepts/marketing-and-strategy-terms/2515-political-environment.html [accessed November 10, 2023].

McKinsey (2023). Supply Chain Resilience – In China and Everywhere Else. Available at: Supply chain resilience—in China and everywhere else (mckinsey.com) [accessed November 22, 2023].

Minkov, M., and Kaasa, A. (2022). Do Dimensions of Culture Exist Objectively? A Validation of the Revised Minkov-Hofstede Model of Culture with World Values Survey Items and Scores for 102 Countries. *Journal of International Management*, Vol. 28, No. 4, 100971.

Mozaffari, M. (2001). The Transformationalist Perspective and the Rise of a Global Standard of Civilization. *International Relations of the Asia-Pacific*, Vol. 1, No. 2, pp. 247–264.

Munck, G.L. (2018). Modernization Theory as a Case of Failed Knowledge Production. *Annals of Comparative Democratization*, Vol. 16, No. 3, pp. 37–41. Available at: https://mk0apsaconnectbvy6p6.kinstacdn.com/wp-content/uploads/sites/26/2018/10/2018 [accessed November 12, 2023].

Nayyar, D. (Ed.) (2002). 6 Cross-border Movements of People. In *Governing Globalization: Issues and Institutions*, WIDER Studies in Development Economics (Oxford, 2002; online edn, Oxford Academic, 3 Oct. 2011), Available at: https://doi.org/10.1093/acprof:oso/9780199254033.003.0006 [accessed December 13, 2024].

NSW Treasury (2022). The Impact of COVID-19 on Global Supply Chain. Available at: Economic data briefing: Global supply chains | NSW Treasury [accessed October 02 2023].

OECD (2011). *OECD Science, Technology and Industry Scoreboard 2011*. Paris: OECD Publishing. http://dx.doi.org/10.1787/sti_scoreboard-2011-en

OECD (2022). OECD Regions and Cities at a Glance 2022. Paris: OECD Publishing. https://doi.org/10.1787/14108660-en

Ouyang, Y. (2022). *Large Countries' Development Path: Experience and Theory*. Berlin: Springer.

Parvati, S. (2022). Dependency Theory: Definition, Approaches, Examples, Limitations. Available at: www.sociologygroup.com/dependency-theory/ [accessed October 02, 2023].

Pew Research Center (2022). Climate Change Remains Top Global Threat Across 19-Country Survey. Available at: Climate Change Remains Top Global Threat Across 19-Country Survey | Pew Research Center [accessed October 02, 2023].

Radović Marković, M., and Tomaš, R. (2019). *Globalization and Entrepreneurship in Small Countries*. New York: Routledge, 174 pp. ISBN 9780367250751.

Ritchie, H., and Roser, M. (2022a). Bangladesh: CO2 Country Profile. Available at: Bangladesh: CO2 Country Profile – Our World in Data [accessed October 14, 2023].

Ritchie, H. and Roser, M. (2022b). Japan: CO2 Country Profile. Available at: Greenhouse gas emissions - Our World in Data

Rosenberg, M. (2019). Geography, Politics, and Economy of Brazil. Available at: Brazil: Geography, Economy, Population [accessed October 02, 2023].

Schiller, H. (1969). *Mass Communication and American Empire*. Boston: Beacon Press.

Schmucler, H. (1975). *Dependencia y Política en la Prensa Argentina, el Caso de LaOpinión. Comunicación y Cambio Social*. Quito, Ecuador: Ciespal.

Shaun, P. (2022). Globalisation Theories: World System, Modernisation, Dependency. Available at: Globalisation Theories: World System, Modernisation, Dependency

Speedtest (October 2023). Japan Median Country Speeds. Available at: Speedtest Global Index – Internet Speed around the world – Speedtest Global Index

Speelman, T. (2022). China's Migration Trends and Policies. Available at: China's Rapid Development Has Transform.. | migrationpolicy.org

State Administration of Foreign Exchange, China (2023). State Administration of Foreign Exchange. Available at: China: Gini coefficient 2005-2023 | Statista

Statista (2023). Inequality of Income Distribution Based on the Gini Coefficient in China from 2012 to 2022. Available at: China: Gini coefficient 2005-2023 | Statista [accessed October 02, 2023].

Steger, M. (2020). 4 The Political Dimension of Globalization. Globalization: A Very Short Introduction. Oxford Academic. Available at: https://doi.org/10.1093/actrade/9780198849452.003.0004

Taylor, P. (2023). Bangladesh: Number of Fixed Broadband Subscriptions 2007–2021. Statista. Available at: Fixed broadband subscriptions in Bangladesh 2007-2022 | Statista [accessed October 02, 2023].

The Economist, (2020). The Yuan Has Been One of the World's Most Stable Major Currencies. Available at: The yuan has been one of the world's most stable major currencies (economist.com) [accessed October 12, 2023].

The Daily Star, (2024). Income inequality in Bangladesh keeps deepening. Avaiable at: Income inequality in Bangladesh keeps deepening | The Daily Star.

The Global Economy.com (2020a). Overall Globalization – Country Rankings. Available at: Overall globalization by country, around the world | TheGlobalEconomy.com

TheGlobalEconomy.com (2020b). Trade Openness. Available at: Trade openness in Asia | TheGlobalEconomy.com [accessed October 02, 2023].

Thomson, K. (2023). The Hyper Globalist View of Globalisation. Available at: The Hyper Globalist View of Globalisation - ReviseSociology [accessed October 07, 2023].

Tomás, P. (2023). China to Reach 1 Billion 5G Subscribers by 2025: GSMA. Available at: China to reach 1 billion 5G subscribers by 2025: GSMA [accessed October 17, 2023].

UNCTAD (2023). World Investment Report. Available at: www.investmentmonitor.ai/news/unctad-world-investment-report-global-foreign-direct-investment-declined-by-11-in-2022/#:~:text=After%20nosediving%20in%202020%20and%20rebounding%20in%202021%2C,a%20flagship%20annual%20publication%20released%20on%204%20July [accessed October 07, 2023].

UNESCO (n.d.). Cultural Exchange Programmes. Available at: Cultural exchange programmes - Policy Monitoring Platform [accessed October 07, 2023].

UN MIGRATION (2022). World Migration Report 2022. Available at: https://worldmigrationreport.iom.int/wmr-2022-interactive/

Urata, S. (2022). Globalization of Japanese Economy: Reality and Impacts. Available at: Globalization of Japanese Economy: Reality and Impacts - WORLD INSIGHT [accessed October 25, 2023].

US Department of State (2022). U.S. Relations With Bangladesh. Available at: U.S. Relations With Bangladesh - United States Department of State [accessed October 07, 2023].

von Kameke, L. (2023). Internet Usage in the Asia-Pacific Region – Statistics & Facts. Statista. Available at: Internet usage in the Asia-Pacific region – statistics & facts | Statista [accessed November 12 2023].

Wallerstein, I., (1993). *Sistemul mondial modern*. Editura Meridiane, Bucurest.

WEF (2021). Facilitating Innovation. Available at: The countries that spend most on research and development | World Economic Forum [accessed November 17, 2023].

Wiest, J.B. (2016). "The Role of Mass Media in the Transmission of Culture", in *Communication and Information Technologies Annual: Media Cultures* (Studies in Media and Communications, Vol. 11). Bingley: Emerald Group, pp. 203–219.

Wolff, J. (2021). How Is Technology Changing the World, and How Should the World Change Technology? Available at: How Is Technology Changing the World, and How Should the World Change Technology? | Global Perspectives | University of California Press (ucpress.edu) [accessed November 17, 2023].

World Population Review (2023a). Income Inequality by Country 2023. Available at: Income Inequality by Country 2024 [accessed March 27, 2024].

World Population Review (2023b). Internet Speeds by Country 2023. Available at: Income Inequality by Country 2024 [accessed March 27, 2024].

World Population Review (2024). Largest Countries in the World 2024. Available at: Total Population by Country 2024 [accessed March 25 2024].

Wu, N. (2015). Income Inequality in China and the Urban-Rural Divide. Available at: Income inequality in China and the urban-rural divide – The Journalist's Resource (journalistsresource.org) [accessed March 27, 2024].

Xu, Y., Zhang, W. (2017). New Media's Impact on China from a Culture Perspective. In: K. Xue, and M. Yu, (Eds.), *New Media and Chinese Society: Communication, Culture and Change in Asia*, vol. 5. Singapore: Springer. https://doi.org/10.1007/978-981-10-6710-5_6

Youmatter (2019). An Official Definition of Globalization by the World Health Organization (WHO). Available at: What is Globalization? Examples, Definition, Benefits and Effects [accessed March 20, 2024].

PART II

The Global Economic Trends

2 China's Role In Globalization

Mirjana Radović-Marković

2.1 China's Position in Global Trends

Since 1978, China has been one of the world's fastest-growing economies due the implementation of economic reforms, with annual growth rates averaging around 10% (World Bank, 2023). However, China began integrating itself into the global economy in the 1990s, when the country's leader, at that moment proposed opening up the country for the first time. Since then, China has become a very important global player. Namely, China, which has around 1.5 billion people (Picture 2.1), sees globalization as an important component in its economic development and for the prospective future.

According to the World Bank (2023), China has become increasingly integrated into the global economy, a process referred to as "globalization." Therefore, globalization has had an important impact on China's economy and society over time. Namely, on the economic front, globalization has helped China achieve rapid economic growth and poverty reduction.

In recent years, China has developed the Country Partnership Framework (CPF), which is a strategic document that outlines the World Bank Group's engagement with a country over a period of time (World Bank, 2019b). The CPF aims to support China's transition to a high-quality, sustainable, and inclusive growth path. The CPF has three strategic objectives: (1) promoting green and low-carbon development, (2) improving social inclusion and public services, and (3) enhancing governance and market efficiency. China has also been working to improve its business environment and has been increasingly welcoming of foreign investment (World Bank, 2019b).

DOI: 10.4324/9781003602378-4

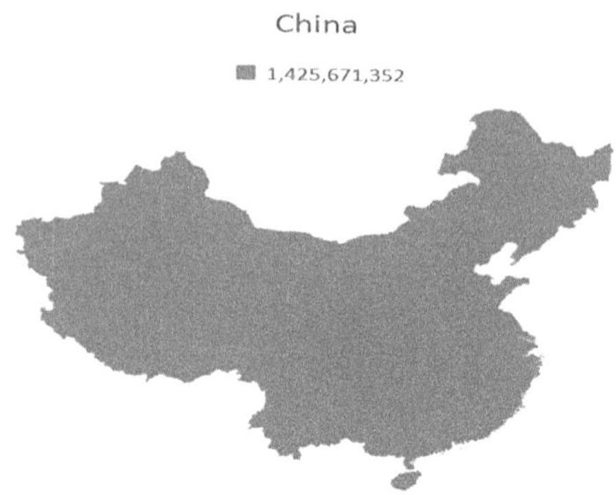

Picture 2.1 China.

Source: Author.

The China Country Partnership Framework for the Period FY2020–2025 is a CPF that outlines the World Bank Group's engagement with China over the period from fiscal year 2020 to fiscal year 2025 (World Bank, 2019a).

The Chinese economy grew significantly after it joined the World Trade Organization (WTO) in 2001. China became the top exporter of merchandise trade in 2020, accounting for 13% of the world's total (up from 12% in 2019), totaling US$ 2,323 billion (WTO, 2021).

The World Trade Statistical Review 2021 by the World Trade Organization also states that China's share of global trade increased from 1.9% in 2000 to 11.4% in 2017 (WTO, 2021).

By 2018, China's goods trade was worth nearly $4.6 trillion, accounting for approximately 12% of total global trade. According to WTO (2021), China's cumulative exports of commercial services between January and April 2021 were up 25% compared with the same period in 2019, more than any other major economy.

The Index of Globalization in China is a metric that assesses China's level of integration and participation in the global economy. It typically includes various indicators related to economic, political, cultural, and social aspects of globalization. These indicators can include trade volume, foreign direct investment, cultural exchange, and more.

The 2022 edition of the Globalization Index by KOF is available for 195 countries and measures the rate of globalization in countries around the world based on three dimensions: economic, social, and political. The KOF Globalisation Index is a measure of the economic, social, and political dimensions of globalization in each country. It was developed by the KOF Swiss Economic Institute at ETH Zurich and has been calculated since 1970 (Statista, 2023).

2.2 Why Has China Been Considered as the Winner of Globalization?

China has been considered one of the winners of globalization for several reasons:

- *Export-Led Growth*: China has become a global manufacturing and export hub, benefiting from globalization by exporting a wide range of goods to markets around the world. This export-driven growth has boosted its economy significantly.
- *Foreign Direct Investment (FDI)*: China has attracted substantial foreign direct investment, which has fueled its economic development and modernization. This investment has come from multinational corporations seeking access to China's vast consumer market and low-cost labor.
- *Integration into Global Supply Chains*: China has positioned itself as a key player in global supply chains, playing a vital role in the production and assembly of various products, from electronics to textiles.
- *Access to Technology and Knowledge*: Through globalization, China has gained access to technology, knowledge, and expertise from around the world, helping it advance in various industries and research areas.
- *Infrastructure Development*: Globalization has supported China's infrastructure development, including transportation, logistics, and communication networks, which has enhanced its connectivity with the global economy.
- *Economic Reform and Liberalization*: China has pursued economic reforms and liberalization policies that align with the principles of globalization, promoting trade and investment.
- *Gross Domestic Product (GDP) per capita*: It is a measure of the economic output of a country divided by its total population. It is

Table 2.1 Globalization Index (KOF): China, Japan and Bangladesh

Country	*2015*	*2016*	*2017*	*2018*	*2019*	*2020*
China	46.05	46.65	47.87	44.95	45.56	45.00
Japan	78.42	78.51	78.81	78.40	48.45	75.00
Bangladesh	51.67	51.43	51.26	50.12	49.33	50.00

Source: Prepared according to The Global Economy.com (2022).

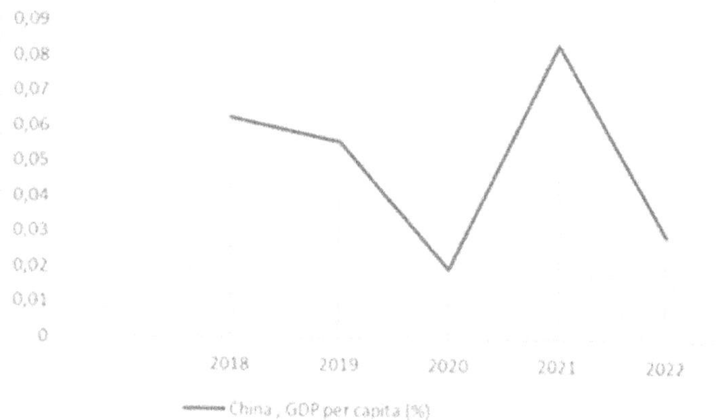

Figure 2.1 China, GDP per capita (%).

Source: Prepared according to The World Bank (2023).

often used as an indicator of a country's standard of living. The GDP per capita in China varies from 2018 to 2022 (Figure 2.1).

According to a report by Boston Consulting Group (BCG), Bangladesh has been experiencing an average annual GDP growth of 6.4% between 2016 and 2021, outpacing Asian peers such as India, Indonesia, and the Philippines, and performing significantly better than the global average of 2.9% (Munir et al., 2023). The country's GDP per capita was ~$2,800 in 2022, which is already higher than India's (Munir et al., 2023). This report also highlights that Bangladesh has a large domestic consumer market, a rapidly expanding middle and affluent class, and an impressive digital adoption rate, which are

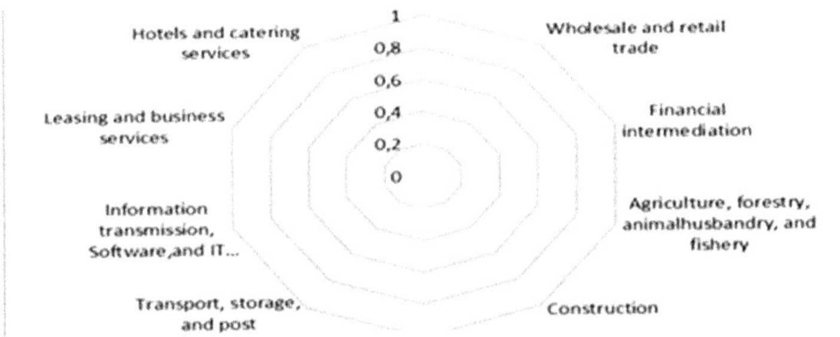

Figure 2.2 Distribution of the gross domestic product (GDP) in China in 2022, by industry.

Source: Author according to data of Statista (2023).

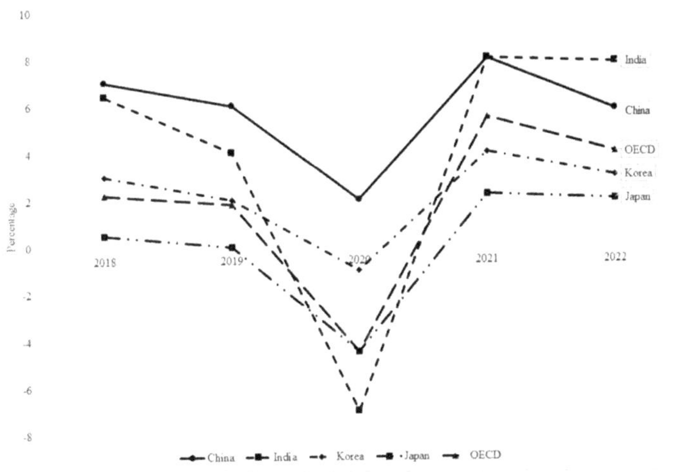

Figure 2.3 Countries experienced a decline in GDP growth with the outbreak of the COVID-19 pandemic (Note: e = estimate; f = forecast).

Source: According to World Bank (2021), World Development Indicators.

driving the country's growth. According to Textor (2023), the industrial sector generated almost 33.2 percent of China's GDP in 2022 (Figure 2.2). Real GDP growth for the Asia region fell markedly at the beginning of the COVID-19 pandemic (Figure 2.3).

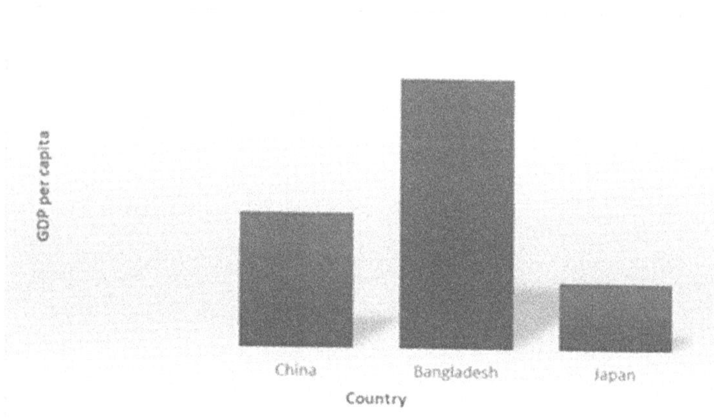

Figure 2.4 GDP per capita growth (annual %) – China, Bangladesh, Japan in 2022.

Source: Author according to data of Statista (2023).

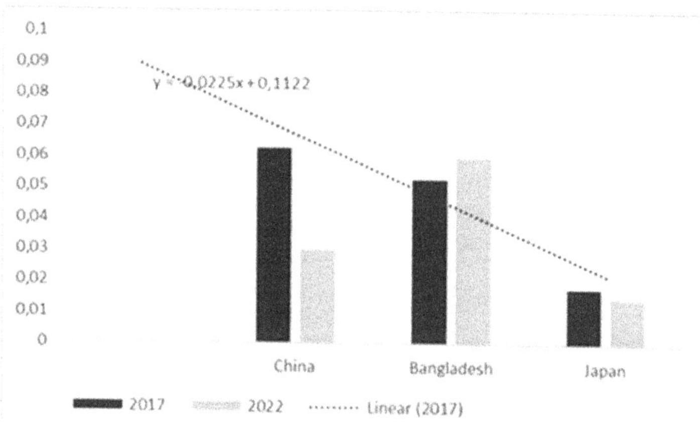

Figure 2.5 GDP per capita growth (annual %) – China, Bangladesh, Japan, 2017–2022.

Source: Author according to data of Statista (2023).

We can note that China's GDP per capita growth rate in 2022 is projected to be significantly lower, while Japan's is projected to be slightly lower than in 2017, just before the outbreak of the COVID-19 pandemic. At the same time, in Bangladesh, GDP growth per capita is higher in 2022 than in 2017 (Figures 2.4 and 2.5).

2.3 China's Role in the Next Phase of Globalization

China's economic progress is directly related to its integration into the global markets. According to Shearing (2022), China has achieved huge benefits from integration by transforming itself into a global manufacturing hub. First of all, it gave China access to global financial markets and access to advanced technology. In addition, the rapid industrialization and urbanization in China established a pathway for millions of people to exit poverty.

China's current status as one of the world's most connected countries is remarkable given that it was a closed economy just four decades ago. Its connection with global business flows can be measured with the help of two significant connectivity indices: MGI and DHL.

- The MGI Connectedness Index and the DHL Global Connectedness Index are two separate indices that measure the connectedness of countries across different flows. The MGI Connectedness Index measures the connectedness of countries across five flows of goods, services, finance, people, and data. On the other hand, the DHL Global Connectedness Index measures globalization based on international flows in four domains: trade, capital, information, and people.
- The latest MGI Connectedness Index report was published in February 2020 and ranks 139 countries on inflows and outflows of goods, services, finance, people, and data. According to this report China accounts for a quarter of global production and is ranked seventh in the MGI Global Connectedness Index. This Index determines how much of a country's trade, capital, information, and people flows are international rather than domestic.
- The latest DHL Global Connectedness Index report was published in March 2023 and ranks 171 countries on their connectedness based on international flows of trade, capital, information, and people (DHL Global Connectedness Index, 2023). According to

> the report, China ranks 31st out of 171 economies in terms of its connectedness, dropping seven notches down since 2019. This report also shows that international flows have been remarkably resilient in the face of recent shocks such as the COVID-19 pandemic and the war in Ukraine. After a slight decline in 2020, the composite DHL Global Connectedness Index rose back to above pre-pandemic levels in 2021. The currently available data points to a further increase in 2022, despite slower growth in some flows (DHL Global Connectedness Index, 2023).

According to our research, China's best interest is to continue to play a leadership role in new global trends as the nation seeks to ensure its own future economic growth and domestic stability.

2.4 How Does Globalization Connect China, Bangladesh and Japan?

Globalization has led to increased trade between these countries. China is known as the "world's factory," and it exports a wide range of goods to Bangladesh and Japan. Bangladesh, in turn, exports garments and textiles to various markets, including Japan. The trade flow has been facilitated by the global supply chain. Globalization has encouraged

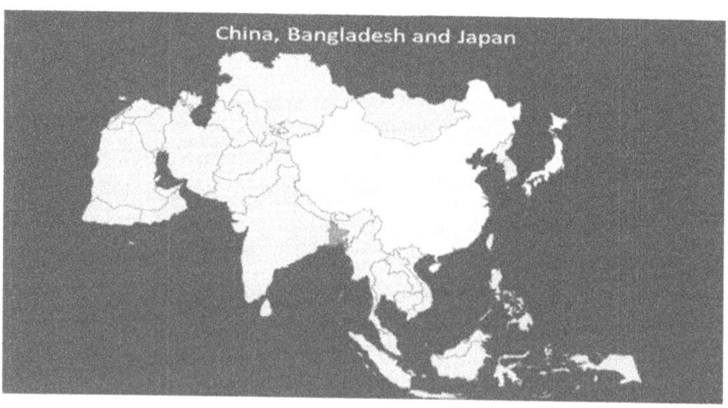

Picture 2.2 Countries in the Region and Their Connection.

Source: Author.

foreign direct investment (FDI) between these countries. Chinese companies invest in Bangladesh and Japan, and Japanese companies have a history of investing in both China and Bangladesh. This cross-border investment helps strengthen economic ties.

China has become a hub for manufacturing and technology, while Japan is known for its advanced technology and innovation. This exchange of ideas and technology benefits all three countries.

Countries in the region, including China, Japan, and Bangladesh, have been involved in regional economic initiatives. For example, China's Belt and Road Initiative (BRI) aims to enhance infrastructure connectivity in Asia, which can benefit neighboring countries like Bangladesh, which is one of the countries that has received significant investment from China under the BRI. According to a report by The Business Standard, China has released $4.45 billion for 35 projects under the BRI in Bangladesh over the last 10 years (TBSnews, n.d.). These projects include investments in the power generation and construction sectors.

Japan is not a member of the BRI (Basu, 2018). However, Japan supports infrastructure projects around the world, including in countries that are part of the BRI. For example, Japan's Overseas Loan (OIL) program is one of the more competitive tools in the infrastructure financing framework (Basu, 2018). In fact, Japan's JBIC (Japan Bank for International Cooperation) is investing in projects around the world, including coal-fired power projects in Vietnam, solar energy projects in the Middle East, and offshore wind projects in the United Kingdom (Basu, 2018). In line with this we can conclude that Japan's support for the BRI is gaining momentum.

According to The Diplomat (Basu, 2018), Japan's support for the BRI is contingent on shaping China into a very important global player. The reason is that Japan saw the need to reduce the economic role of the United States in Asia. In this context, Japan has supported China's initiatives, particularly when it comes to promoting the development of the region's middle-income countries.

Finally, we can conclude that Japan and Bangladesh have maintained a warm relationship for over 50 years, which can be dubbed as a "good model" of development partnership.

2.5 Conclusion

The unitary globalized economy no longer exists. Therefore, a new and more diverse globalization is both required and being built. "The transition is ongoing, and its final form is yet to be determined" (Kramer, 2023).

Globalization is a complex phenomenon that has a significant impact on countries of all sizes. The influence of globalization on large countries depends on several factors, including their economic, political, and social systems. Developed nations benefit from globalization in production, international trade, and the financial markets.

It allows businesses or other organizations to create influence and develop operations in many regions. It combines gross domestic product (GDP), industrialization, and the Human Development Index (HDI).

Globalization has both advantages and challenges for large countries, impacting their economies, cultures, politics, and environment. How a large country navigates these effects depends on its policies and strategies in response to the opportunities and challenges presented by globalization.

China has become an increasingly important player in the global economy and politics in recent years. As its economy expands, the world's most populous nation is branching out in efforts ranging from transportation infrastructure expansion in Asia—known as the Belt and Road Initiative—to significant investment in Africa and South America. China is also a major player in international trade, with the world's second largest population and the second-largest economy in the world. China's status as the second-largest economy in the world (as measured by GDP) continues to position it as an important player on the global economic stage. China is no longer just a rising power; it is now a truly global actor economically. China will continue to play an important role in the new globalization in the future.

In conclusion, the influence of globalization on large countries is a multifaceted issue that depends on various factors. It fosters cultural exchange, including through media, tourism, and educational opportunities. This allows people from China, Bangladesh, and Japan to better understand and appreciate each other's cultures.

References

Basu, T. (2018). Japan's Belt and Road Puzzle, Decoded. Available at: The Diplomat-Japan s Belt and Road Puzzle Decoded-Titli Basu.pdf [accessed March 27, 2024].

DHL Global Connectedness Index (2023). Globalization Resilient even as U.S.-China Decoupling Advances. Available at: Mar 15, 2023: DHL Global Connectedness Index: Globalization resilient even as U.S.-China decoupling advances - DHL Group [accessed March 27, 2024].

Kramer, F. (2023). *China and the New Globalization.* The Scowcroft Center for Strategy and Security. China and the new globalization, Atlantic Council.

Munir, Z., Chakraborty, S., and Ishtiaque, T (2023). Bangladesh's Economy Is Growing, and So Are Its Emerging Champions. Available at: Growth in Bangladesh's Economy and Emerging Champions | BCG [accessed March 27, 2024].

Shearing, N. (2022). China Is One of Globalisation's Winners. It Won't Throw That Away for Russia. Capital Economics. Available at: China is one of globalisation's winners. It won't throw that away for Russia. | Capital Economics [accessed March 23, 2024].

Statista (2024). Top 50 Countries in the Globalization Index 2022. Available at: Globalization Index by country 2023 | Statista [accessed March 27 2024].

TBSnews (n.d.). Belt and Road Initiative: China Releases $4.45b in 10 Years for Bangladesh. Available at: Belt and Road Initiative: China releases $4.45b in 10 years for Bangladesh | The Business Standard [accessed March 20, 2024].

World Bank (2019a). China – Country Partnership Framework for the Period FY2020-2025. Available at: China - Country Partnership Framework for the Period FY2020-2025 [accessed March 20, 2024].

World Bank (2019b). Country Partnership Framework for the People's Republic of China for the Period FY2020-2025, November 11. Available at: World Bank Document [accessed March 21, 2024].

World Bank (2021). Gini Index – Japan. Available at: Gini index – Japan | Data (worldbank.org) [accessed March 20, 2024].

World Bank (2023). The World Bank in China. Available at: China-Economic-Update-Dec23-EN.pdf

WTO (2021). World Trade Statistical Review 2021. Available at: WTO | Trade Statistics - World Trade Statistical Review 2021 (WTSR 2021) [accessed March 27, 2024].

PART III

The Digital Transformation of Entrepreneurship and Education

Economic Effects

3 Digital Economy

Mirjana Radović-Marković

3.1 Introduction

The digital economy is the part of the economy that is based on digital technologies, such as the internet, cloud computing, artificial intelligence, and e-commerce. It includes various sectors, such as online retail, digital media, digital finance, digital education, and digital health. Digitization is moving most business processes into the virtual sphere. The digitized companies and new concepts of organizational functioning are our new reality (Radović-Marković, et.al., 2021).

The digital economy uses a wide range of industries and activities that utilize digital technologies and platforms. Employment in the digital economy can vary across countries and regions. According to a report by the China Academy of Information and Communications Technology, the market size of China's digital economy grew from 31.3 to 50.2 trillion yuan (about $7.25 trillion) in the period between 2018 and 2022 (Table 3.1), with a year-on-year nominal growth of 10.3% (Statista, 2024). This accounted for 42% of China's gross domestic product (GDP) (SDG, 2024). Further, China ranked second in the world in terms of digital economy size, behind only the United States (chinadaily.com.cn, 2021).

The report also highlighted the key drivers of China's digital economy growth, such as the rapid development of 5G networks, the widespread adoption of cloud computing and big data, the innovation of digital platforms and applications, and the improvement of digital infrastructure and governance.

The aim of this chapter is to show that digital transformation of organization is driven by the evolution of the new digital technology.

DOI: 10.4324/9781003602378-6

Table 3.1 Market Size of the Digital Economy in China (2018–2022)

Year	*2018*	*2019*	*2020*	*2021*	*2022*	*2023*
Market size in trillion yuan	31.30	35.80	39.20	45.50	50.20	53.90

Source: Author prepared according to Statista (2023).

3.2 Economic Effects of Artificial Intelligence (AI) on the Economy and Society in China, Japan and Bangladesh

Artificial Intelligence (AI) has the potential to make a significant impact on the economy and society. AI can increase the efficiency with which things are done, vastly improve the decision-making process by analyzing large amounts of data, and spawn the creation of new products and services, markets, and industries, thereby boosting consumer demand and generating new revenue streams. According to a report by PriceWaterhouseCoopers, AI technologies could increase global GDP by $15.7 trillion, a full 14%, by 2030 (West and Allen, 2018). According to a report by the McKinsey Global Institute (2018), leading countries could capture an additional 20–25% in net economic benefits compared with today, while developing countries may capture only about 5–15%.

There are many companies that are using AI in the current world. According to a report by Fast Company, some of the most innovative companies in AI include OpenAI, DeepMind, Nvidia, Builder.ai, Voxel, and others (Ufberg, 2023).

IMARC Group has made a list of the top 17 artificial intelligence companies in the world, including Amazon Web Services Inc., Apple Inc., Baidu, Cisco Systems Inc., Facebook Inc., General Electric Company, Google LLC (Alphabet Inc.), International Business Machines, Intel Corporation, Micron Technology Inc., Microsoft Corporation, Nvidia Corporation, Oracle Corporation, Rockwell Automation Inc., and Samsung Electronics Co.

Artificial Intelligence (AI) is being used extensively in Bangladesh, China, India, and Japan. In India, AI is being used in various sectors such as healthcare, finance, and education, among others. For instance, AI is being used to predict and prevent diseases, improve customer service, and enhance the quality of education (Pandit, 2021). In Japan, AI and robotics are being used to solve social issues and achieve economic growth. For example, robots are being used to take on repetitive jobs in the manufacturing line, such as filling boxes or welding a car frame. China has been investing heavily in artificial intelligence (AI) and aims to become the world leader in AI by 2030 (Elliot, 2020). The country is making rapid progress in AI research, and central and local government spending on AI in China is estimated to be in the tens of billions of dollars. China's AI sector has seen outsized success, with Chinese companies producing the most accurate facial recognition technology (DeSmith, 2023). According to DeSmith (2023), the Chinese government is installing facial recognition equipment across entrances to many of its subway stations. A report from Stanford University detailed that China is at the forefront of AI development. It has also noted that the development of AI is a national priority. The country is investing heavily in AI research and development, with the highest number of AI startups and the most significant number of AI patents in the world. The AI market size in China reached $12.9 billion by 2022 (Slotta, 2023).

Artificial Intelligence (AI) is a rapidly growing field in Bangladesh. Bangladesh is at the very beginning of using artificial intelligence. However, there is huge potential for using artificial intelligence. AI is being applied in various industries such as ride-sharing, natural language processing (NLP) for Bengali, ChatBots, booking hotels, buying air tickets, and real-time mapping, among others (Babu, 2021). According to a report by the Centre for Policy Dialogue, Bangladesh has set a developmental approach towards research and development, skilling and reskilling of AI workforce, data and digital infrastructure, ethics, data privacy, security and regulations, funding and accelerating AI start-ups, and industrialization for AI technologies (Khatun and Nawrin, 2021). The report also highlights that AI can be used in various domains, from farming to manufacturing, hospitality to healthcare, public services to professional services, judiciary to defense, and others (Bari, 2021).

According to the National Strategy for Artificial Intelligence Bangladesh report, Bangladesh is embracing AI for the digitalization of the nation. The digitization process started a decade ago, and now AI is expected to work as an accelerator. The report states that Bangladesh aims to transform itself into a technologically-advanced nation by 2030 and leverage ICT as a tool for sustainable development. The report also highlights that AI has a great impact on the economy as well as offering substantial benefits. If repetitive tasks and the role of humans can be automated, this will increase GDP gain and improve labor productivity.

It is important to note that AI is not only taking over the routine back-office roles or blue-collar jobs but also threatening to pervade the cognitive domain that has traditionally been under human control for thousands of years (Bari, 2021). As AI penetrates every sphere of human life, it is imperative for us to formulate a roadmap to see the opportunities and identify its likely threats.

3.3 Impact of New Technologies on Creative Destruction

The impact of new technologies on creative destruction is a complex and multifaceted topic. Creative destruction refers to the process in which new innovations and technologies disrupt existing industries, leading to the decline or obsolescence of established businesses and the creation of new ones. Here are some theories and perspectives on this impact:

- ***Schumpeterian Theory***: Joseph Schumpeter's (1942) theory of creative destruction suggests that technological innovation is the driving force behind economic growth. New technologies disrupt existing markets and business models, leading to the replacement of old industries with new ones, ultimately fostering economic progress (Kopp, 2023).
- ***Disruption Theory***: Harvard professor Christensen's theory (Christensen, 1997), of disruptive innovation explains how new technologies often start in niche markets or lower-end segments, gradually improving and expanding their capabilities until they disrupt established markets and businesses. This theory highlights the gradual and unforeseen nature of creative destruction.
- ***Job Displacement***: While new technologies can create new job opportunities, they can also displace workers in traditional industries. Some argue that automation and artificial intelligence may lead to job losses in certain sectors, potentially exacerbating income inequality. A report by Brookings suggests that the "new automation" of the next few decades—with much more advanced robotics and artificial intelligence (AI)—will widen the range of tasks and jobs that machines can perform, and have the potential to cause much more worker displacement and inequality than older generations of automation (Holzer, 2022). A study by MIT News

found that automation accounts for more than half of the increase in income inequality between more- and less-educated workers over the last four decades (Dizikes, 2022). It is important to note that while AI has the potential to create new opportunities, it is also important to address the potential negative impacts on the workforce and society as a whole.

- ***Market Dynamics***: New technologies can change market dynamics by altering consumer behavior and preferences. Namely, the rise of e-commerce has transformed the retail industry, with consumers shifting from brick-and-mortar stores to online shopping. For instance, the widespread adoption of smartphones has led to a shift in consumer behavior, with more people using mobile devices to access the internet and make purchases (Hernandez, 2021). According to Deloitte's 2019 global mobile consumer survey, in most developed markets, about 90% of adults own a smartphone, with around 95% of those smartphones used daily (Lee et al., 2021). As a result of its phenomenal success, the smartphone market has reached maturity, with adoption levels nearing their natural plateau in most developed markets. Similarly, the rise of social media has enabled consumers to interact with brands in new ways, leading to changes in consumer preferences.
- ***Regulatory Challenges***: The process of "creative destruction," whereby new technologies and business models displace old ones, is key to growth and innovation. Creative destruction can pose regulatory challenges. Governments may struggle to adapt existing regulations to new technologies, leading to issues related to privacy, security, and competition. However, it is important to note that creative destruction may be inevitable, but it must not be achieved too easily, or innovators will not have enough incentive to enter the market (Baslandze, 2021). In fact, a recent study by Baslandze (2021) found that patent protection is positively associated with the number of firms entering the market. This suggests that patent laws and intellectual property right legislations can be effective in promoting competition and innovation. Ensuring that innovators profit from their innovations is the object of patent laws and intellectual property right legislations.
- ***Sustainability***: The impact of new technologies on creative destruction also raises questions about sustainability. While innovation can lead to more efficient and sustainable practices, it can also contribute to resource depletion and environmental concerns (WEF,

2022). According to WEF (2022), digital technologies are being used to measure a sustainability progress, more efficient use of resources and to reduce greenhouse gas emissions. It is important to strike a balance between innovation and sustainability to ensure a better future for our planet.

- ***Economic Growth***: Many economists argue that creative destruction is essential for long-term economic growth. It encourages businesses to innovate and adapt, driving productivity gains and overall prosperity. According to a study by researchers Garcia-Macia, Hsieh, and Klenow (2017), while creative destruction plays a vital role in driving economic growth, it is not the dominant force. They believe that creative destruction accounts for only about 25% of growth, while product refinement and quality improvement account for much more. Many developing countries seek to improve the policy frameworks, technical programs, skills development programs, and financing initiatives that support entrepreneurship in the digital economy. The ultimate aim of these initiatives is to improve competitiveness, attract investment, create jobs, and grow markets.
- ***Disruption in Creative Industries***: In creative industries like music, film, and publishing, digital technologies have drastically disrupted traditional distribution models. This has both positive and negative consequences for content creators and consumers. According to a report by the European Commission (2021), digitalization has transformed the processes of creation, production, distribution, and consumption of content. Culture is increasingly accessed through dedicated platforms, applications, social media, and aggregators. Moreover, digitization has disrupted the traditional value chains of creative industries and led to more complexity.
- ***Intellectual Property***: The digital age has challenged traditional concepts of intellectual property, leading to debates about copyright, piracy, and the protection of creative works in the era of easily replicable digital content. The ease of copying and sharing digital content has made it difficult for creators to protect their work from unauthorized use and distribution. This has led to a rise in piracy and illegal distribution of copyrighted material, which has had a significant impact on the creative industry. For example, the World Intellectual Property Organization (WIPO) has developed international treaties to harmonize copyright law among nations (Shuvo, n.d.).

- ***Social and Cultural Impact***: Creative destruction can have profound social and cultural effects. It can change how people interact, consume media, and engage in various aspects of life. Creative destruction is a term coined by economist Schumpeter to describe the process of innovation that disrupts existing industries and creates new ones (Kopp, 2023). It can have profound social and cultural effects, changing how people interact, consume media, and engage in various aspects of life. Coastal sea-level rise, inefficient resource and land use, and the role of the built environment in perpetuating social exclusion raise questions about the potential value of destruction and the opportunities it affords for reframing spatial memory and historical narrative in more just and sustainable ways (Avrami, 2020). However, creative destruction can also have negative social consequences, such as job loss and economic instability (Kopp, 2023). The heritage field's preoccupation with the physical, place-based fabric will be challenged in the face of this obsolescence, compelling a reexamination of attitudes toward destruction and reconstruction. It is important to consider both the positive and negative aspects of creative destruction when evaluating its social and cultural impact.

The impact of new technologies on creative destruction varies across industries and regions, and it is an ongoing area of study and debate. It is important for policymakers, businesses, and society as a whole to navigate these changes thoughtfully to maximize the benefits of innovation while addressing its challenges.

3.4 Digital Entrepreneurship

Digital entrepreneurship is a rapidly growing field, and its development varies across different countries. This term used to describe the act of establishing new companies specifically in the digital economy (Mailchimp, n.d.). While global entrepreneurship focuses on expanding a business across borders, digital entrepreneurship focuses on leveraging digital technologies to create and improve businesses.

It is a term that describes how entrepreneurship will change as business and society continue to be transformed by digital technology. Digital entrepreneurship involves the use of digital technologies and the internet to create, manage, and grow businesses. It allows entrepreneurs to reach a global audience and use organic marketing tactics to build their customer base without spending a fortune, (Mailchimp, n.d.). It involves using digital technologies to create new business models, products, and services, and to improve existing ones. Digital entrepreneurship highlights changes in entrepreneurial practice, theory, and education (Chakravorti and Chaturvedi, 2019).

A Harvard Business Program article ranked 42 countries by ease of doing digital business and found that Singapore has the world's best digital entrepreneurship system, followed by the United States, Sweden, Denmark, and Switzerland (Chakravorti and Chaturvedi, 2019). The Asian Development Bank also reports that Singapore has the best digital entrepreneurship system, followed by the United States, Sweden, Denmark, and Switzerland (ScandAsia, 2024).

The World Bank has published a report on increasing entrepreneurship in the digital economy, which highlights the importance of improving policy frameworks, technical programs, skills development programs, and financing initiatives that support entrepreneurship in the digital economy.

3.5 The Digital Entrepreneurship Index (DEI)

The Digital Entrepreneurship Index (DEI) is a composite index that measures the quality of the digital entrepreneurship ecosystem in a country. It is based on four pillars: digital infrastructure governance, digital user citizenship, digital technology entrepreneurship, and digital multisided platforms. A study conducted by the Global Entrepreneurship and Development Institute (GEDI) found a positive correlation between the DEI score and GDP per capita.

According to Asian Development Outlook (2022), China is positioned as 13th in the list of countries with score of 35.3 in 2021 (Table 3.2). However, Bangladesh ranks 96th among 113 economies in the Global Index of Digital Entrepreneurship Systems. The index is prepared by looking at the level of digitalization in eight areas: culture and informal institutions; formal institutions, regulation, and taxation; market conditions; physical infrastructure; human capital; knowledge creation and dissemination; finance; and networking and support. Bangladesh is the fourth weakest among the 21 ADB member economies, with its very poor performance in three areas: culture and informal institutions, market conditions, and human capital. The overall score of the country is only 12.5 out of 100 in the index (TBSnews, 2022). ADB Chief Economist Albert Park said, "Digital

Table 3.2 Global Index of Digital Entrepreneurship Systems 2021 Scores

Country	*Score (0–100)*
Singapore	81.30
United States	79.70
Sweden	79.60
Denmark	78.80
Switzerland	76.90
Netherlands	75.60
Finland	73.30
Norway	69.90
Luxembourg	69.60
United Kingdom	69.00
Republic of Korea	54.10
Malaysia	43.10
China	35.30

Source: Prepared according to Asian Development Bank (Asian Development Outlook, 2022).

entrepreneurship helped economies stay afloat during the Covid-19 pandemic, and it can become a major engine of growth and innovation in the post-pandemic world." "For this to happen, there needs to be a supportive environment enabled by conducive policies and incentives" (TBSnews, 2022). One of the reasons for Bangladesh's low ranking is its poor performance in the areas of culture and informal institutions, market conditions, and human capital

Statistical data in Japan also showed that digital entrepreneurship is on the rise. In this context, a report from the Ministry of Economy, Trade and Industry showed that the number of new businesses in Japan increased by 4.5% in 2020, with a significant portion of these being digital startups (Asian Development Outlook, 2020). The report also highlights the importance of digital transformation for small and medium-sized enterprises (SMEs) in Japan, which can help them to improve their competitiveness and resilience.

The China Digital Economy Innovation and Entrepreneurship Index (IRIEDEC) is a set of indices that evaluate the development level of the digital economy in different regions of China. The index system focuses on the innovation and entrepreneurship behavior of enterprise entities, and evaluates the development level of the digital economy in different regions of China (Dai, Wang, and Zhang, 2021).

A report by Accenture (2022) provides insights into the digital transformation of Chinese companies in 2022. The report shows that Chinese companies have been making progress in digital transformation over the past five years. Notably, 17% of these companies, referred to as "Champions," have made decisive investments in adopting and scaling digital technologies to drive continuous business transformation/

This trend has seen a substantial increase compared to just 7% in 2018 (Accenture.com, 2022). The research also shows that there has been a slight 1% increase in the number of companies qualifying as champions since 2021, however the average score measuring digital proficiency declined for the first time in five years from 54 to 52 between 2021 to 2022, out of a total achievable score of 100 (Accenture.com, 2022).

According to a report by the European Center for Digital Competitiveness, China has made significant strides in digital competitiveness over the past three years, ranking second among the G20 countries (WEF, 2021). The report analyzed the digital competitiveness of 140 countries and provided a global ranking that compared them within their regions. The ranking revealed strong dynamics regarding the two global digital superpowers: China gained significantly in digital competitiveness, while the US lost out over the same time period, mainly driven by the ecosystem dimension in the ranking (WEF, 2021).

The implementation of new technologies often leads to creative destruction, where established industries and products are disrupted and replaced by innovative ones. The future of this process will likely continue to be shaped by emerging technologies such as AI, automation, blockchain, and biotechnology. These technologies can revolutionize various industries, creating both opportunities and challenges. Adaptation, regulation, and ethical considerations will play crucial roles in how creative destruction unfolds in the coming years. Ultimately, it's a complex and dynamic process that will reshape the economic and technological landscape. In addition, digital technologies have transformed the reskilling landscape by making learning more accessible, personalized, and adaptable to the needs of individuals and industries, promoting a lifelong learning mindset.

3.6 The Digital Transformation of Higher Education

Digital technologies have been a catalyst for creative destruction in various industries. They have disrupted existing routines and structures while creating new opportunities for innovation. Through creative destruction, digital technologies fundamentally challenge existing routines, capabilities, and structures by which organizations presently operate, adapt, and innovate.

The origins of modern technological change provide the context necessary to understand present-day technological transformation, to investigate the impact of the new digital technologies, and to examine the phenomenon of digital disruption of established industries and occupations. How these contemporary technologies will transform industries and institutions, or serve to create new industries and institutions, will unfold in time. The implications of the relationships between these pervasive new forms of digital transformation and the accompanying new business models, business strategies, innovation, and capabilities are being worked through at global, national, corporate, and local levels. Whatever the technological future holds it will be defined by continual adaptation, perpetual innovation, and the search for new potential.

The Chinese government is committed to building the national smart education platform into an important public service product in the field of education, promoting the integration and development of digital technology and traditional education, and calling on all countries to work together to carry forward their fine traditions and promote innovation, for digital education to benefit people of all countries (WEF, 2020).

China has been making significant efforts to promote digital education in recent years. The Chinese government has released multiple plans to better apply information technology to education, calling for the digitalization of education and the building of a society and country of learning in which lifelong learning is pursued by all. The government has also been investing in improving connectivity, particularly in rural and inland areas, to address the digital divide between China's cities and rural areas (Chan, 2013). The Chinese government values the development of digital education as an important component of digital China.

After years of continuous efforts, China's educational informatization has achieved a leap-forward in development, with 100% internet access on campus and 99.5% of primary and secondary schools equipped with multimedia classrooms (www.moe.gov.cn, 2023).

Japan has been investing in digital education for many years. The country has a well-established digital education system that includes online courses, e-learning platforms, and digital textbooks.

The Japanese government has been promoting digital education as a way to improve the quality of education and to address the declining birthrate and aging population.

In 2020, the Japanese government launched a new initiative called the "Digital Transformation of Education" to accelerate the adoption of digital technology in education. Japan has been taking steps to digitize its education system. The Japanese government has been promoting ICT-based education to raise children who are empowered to think and act on their own by leveraging the power of digital devices. In this context, in 2019, the Japanese government initiated the Global and Innovation Gateway for All (GIGA) School Program, which aimed to equip elementary and junior high schools with computer devices and a high-speed communications network (Kizuna, 2021). The program was accelerated in response to the COVID-19 pandemic, and from April 2023, nearly all schools in Japan will provide a learning environment in which every student has an ICT device. In 2020, the Japanese government launched a new initiative called the "Digital Transformation of Education" to accelerate the adoption of digital technology in education.

At last, the country has a well-established digital education system that includes online courses, e-learning platforms, and digital textbooks.

The Higher Education Quality Enhancement Project (HEQEP) was initiated in 2009 to digitize higher education in Bangladesh. The project aims to improve the quality of teaching and learning in higher education institutions through the use of information and communication technology (ICT) (Mustahsin-Ul-Aziz, 2020). In addition, the COVID-19 pandemic has accelerated the digitization of education in Bangladesh. The government moved quickly to digitalize education wherever possible and introduced TV-based learning for citizens without internet access. This model has benefits for emerging economies that will last well beyond the pandemic itself.

3.7 Conclusion

The digital economy can play an important role in encouraging inclusion and alleviating poverty, for example, by reducing information asymmetries for poor or rural workers, and by fostering entry into the productive labor force of women and younger workers. Young people, consistently the first to embrace new digital technologies, often seek employment in high-tech sectors and can be critical to developing a skilled workforce that is internationally competitive in an increasingly interconnected world. The digital economy is vital to spurring the overall innovation potential of a country in areas such as research and development (R&D), high-tech industry development, and technology patent activity (Fukuda, 2020). For a company to be successful in digital transformation, it must consider the development of many interrelated factors, such as business mobility, infrastructure, data security, customer service, and the ability to constantly change and adapt. Workforce transformation and education are intricately linked to the global economy. By enabling individuals to acquire new skills, fostering lifelong learning, and adapting education systems to meet the demands of the labor market, societies can effectively navigate the challenges and opportunities presented by the changing nature of work. Embracing these transformations can lead to a more skilled, adaptable, and inclusive workforce that drives economic prosperity.

According to the International Labor Organization (ILO), the number of people employed in the digital sector is estimated to be around 1.7 billion (ILO, 2021). The ILO's World Employment and Social Outlook 2021 report explores how the contemporary platform economy is transforming the way work is organized, and analyzes the impact of digital labor platforms on enterprises, workers, and society as a whole. By 2025 there will be 149 million new digital jobs in areas like privacy and trust, cybersecurity, data analysis, machine learning and AI, cloud and data roles, and software development (Financial Market, 2020). Therefore, it is not surprising that many organizations, under the threat of digitalization, are trying to introduce new technologies into their business system as soon as possible.

References

Accenture.com (2022). Accenture China Digital Transformation Index 2022. Available at: Accenture China Digital Transformation Index 2022 | Accenture [accessed March 27, 2024].

Avrami, E. (2020). Creative Destruction and the Social (Re) Construction of Heritage. Cambridge University Press.

Babu, K.E.K. (2021). Artificial Intelligence, Its Applications in Different Sectors and Challenges: Bangladesh Context. In: R. Montasari and H. Jahankhani (Eds.), *Artificial Intelligence in Cyber Security: Impact and Implications. Advanced Sciences and Technologies for Security Applications*. Cham: Springer. https://doi.org/10.1007/978-3-030-88040-8_4

Bari, M.A. (2021). Bangladesh in the age of Artificial Intelligence. Available at: Bangladesh in the age of Artificial Intelligence | The Daily Star [accessed March 05, 2024].

Baslandze, S. (2021). Barriers to Creative Destruction: Large Firms and Non-Productive Strategies. CEPR Discussion Paper No. DP16570. Available at SSRN: https://ssrn.com/abstract=3928884 [accessed March 29, 2024].

Chakravorti, B., and Chaturvedi, R.S. (2019). Ranking 42 Countries by Ease of Doing Digital Business. *Harvard Business Review*. Available at: Ranking 42 Countries by Ease of Doing Digital Business | Harvard Business Publishing Education [accessed April 06, 2024].

Chan, J. (2013). Digital Education in China. Available at: Digital education in China | British Council [accessed April 06, 2024].

chinadaily.com.cn. (2021). World's top 10 countries in digital economy. Available at: World's top 10 countries in digital economy – Chinadaily.com.cn [accessed April 07, 2024].

Christensen, C. (1997). *The Innovator's Dilemma*. Cambridge, MA: Harvard Business School Press.

Dai, R., Wang, A., Chen, B., and Zhang, X. (2021). Index of Regional Innovation and Entrepreneurship in Digital Economy in China (IRIEDEC). Peking University Open Research Data Platform, V4. Available at: https://doi.org/10.18170/DVN/EYCVSP.

DeSmith, C. (2023). Why China Has Edge on AI, What Ancient Emperors Tell Us about Xi Jinping. Harvard Gazette. Available at: Why China has an edge on artificial intelligence — Harvard Gazette [accessed April 06, 2024].

Dizikes, P. (2022). Study: Automation Drives Income Inequality. Available at: Study: Automation drives income inequality | MIT News | Massachusetts Institute of Technology [accessed April 08, 2023].

Elliot, H. (2020). China and AI: What the World Can Learn and What It Should Be Wary of. Available at: China and AI: what the world can learn and what it should be wary of (theconversation.com) [accessed April 06, 2024].

European Commission (2021). Transforming the Creative and Cultural Industries with Advanced Technologies. Available at: Leaflet Technological trends in the creative industries.pdf (europa.eu) [accessed April 16, 2024].

Financial Market (2020). 149 Million New Technology Jobs Will Be Created by 2025: This Is How Microsoft Plans to Train Digital Skills. Available at: Financial Market [accessed April 10, 2024].

Fukuda, K. (2020). Science, Technology and Innovation Ecosystem Transformation toward Society 5.0. *Production Economics*, Vol. 220. https://doi.org/10.1016/j.ijpe.2019.07.033

Garcia-Macia, D., Hsieh, C., and Klenow, P. (2017). How Destructive Is Innovation? Available at: Does Creative Destruction Really Drive Economic Growth? | NBER [accessed April 16, 2024].

Hernandez, J. (2021). Three Major Consumer Behavior Shifts Driving the Future of Customer Experiences. Available at: www.forbes.com/sites/forbestechcouncil/2021/10/07/three-major-consumer-behavior-shifts-driving-the-future-of-customer-experiences/?sh=5f9c4db2480e [accessed April 07, 2024].

Holzer, H. (2022). Understanding the Impact of Automation on Workers, Jobs and Wages. Available at: Understanding the impact of automation on workers, jobs, and wages | Brookings [accessed April 06, 2024].

ILO (2021). The Role of Digital Labour Platforms in Transforming the World of Work. Available at: World Employment and Social Outlook 2021: The role of digital labour platforms in transforming the world of work (ilo.org) [accessed April 19, 2023].

Khatun, F., and Nawrin, N. (2021). Impact of Artificial Intelligence in Bangladesh's IT Sector. *The Financial Express*. Available at: Impact of Artificial Intelligence in Bangladesh's IT sector – Fahmida Khatun and Nadia Nawrin | CPD [accessed April 06, 2024].

Kizuna, (2021). ICT in Schools Equips Students with Life Skills for Digital Era. Available at: ICT in Schools Equips Students with Life Skills for Digital Era | The Government of Japan - JapanGov

Kopp, C. (2023). Creative Destruction: Out With the Old, in With the New. Available at: Creative Destruction: Out With the Old, in With the New (investopedia.com) [accessed April 06, 2024].

Lee, P., Casey, M., Wigginton, C., and Calugar-Pop, C. (2021). Deloitte's 2019 Global Mobile Consumer Survey. Available at: DI_2019-global-mobile-survey.pdf [accessed April 06, 2024].

Mailchimp (n.d.). What is Digital Entrepreneurship? And How To Start a Digital Business. Available at: What is Digital Entrepreneurship? Definition & Tips | Mailchimp [accessed April 16 2024].

McKinsey Global Institute (2018). Notes from the AI Frontier Modeling the Impact of AI on the World Economy. Available at: MGI-Notes-from-the-AI-frontier-Modeling-the-impact-of-AI-on-the-world-economy-September-2018.ashx (mckinsey.com) [accessed April 02 2024].

Mustahsin-Ul-Aziz, S. (2020). Covid-19 Boosts Digitization of Higher Education in Bangladesh. Available at: COVID-19 boosts digitization of higher education in Bangladesh (worldbank.org) [accessed March 05, 2024].

Pandit, H. (2021). Using Artificial Intelligence: Bangladesh Has a Long Way to Go. Available at: Using artificial intelligence: Bangladesh has a long way to go | The Business Standard (tbsnews.net) [accessed March 07, 2024].

Radović-Marković, M., Djukanović, B., Marković, D., and Dragojević, A. (2021). *Entrepreneurship and Work in the Gig Economy: The Case of the Western Balkan*. New York: Routledge.

Schumpeter, J.A. (1942). *Capitalism, Socialism, and Democracy.* New York: Harper & Row.

SDG, (2024).How China's digital ecosystem is moving ahead of the rest. Available at: How China's digital ecosystem is moving ahead of the rest | Sekkei Digital Group [accessed March 06, 2024].

Shuvo, S.B. (n.d). Privacy vs. Copyright Protection. Available at: Piracy vs. Copyright Protection: Analyzing the Creative Industry of Bangladesh – FutureLaw (futrlaw.org) [accessed March 06, 2024].

Slotta, D. (2023). Artificial Intelligence in China – Statistics & Facts. Available at: Artificial intelligence in China – statistics & facts | Statista [accessed March 05, 2024].

Statista (2024). Market size of the digital economy in China in selected years from 2005 to 2023 (in trillion yuan). Available at: China: digital economy size 2023 | Statista

TBSnews (2022). Digital Entrepreneurship System: Bangladesh 96th among 113 Economies. Available at: Digital entrepreneurship system: Bangladesh 96th among 113 economies | The Business Standard (tbsnews.net) [accessed March 28, 2024].

Ufberg, M. (2023). The 10 Most Innovative Companies in Artificial Intelligence of 2023. Available at: The 10 most innovative companies in artificial intelligence of 2023 (fastcompany.com) [accessed March 28, 2024].

WEF (2020). Digital Education Is Both a Necessity and an Advantage for the Global South. Here's Why. Available at: How digital education can boost growth in the Global South | World Economic Forum (weforum.org) [accessed March 29, 2024].

WEF (2021). These Countries Rank Highest for Digital Competitiveness. Available at: These countries rank highest for digital competitiveness | World Economic Forum (weforum.org) [accessed March 28, 2024].

WEF (2022). 3 Ways Digital Technology Can Be a Sustainability Game-Changer. Available at: How digital technology can improve your sustainability game | World Economic Forum (weforum.org) [accessed March 29, 2024].

West, D., and Allen, J. (2018). How Artificial Intelligence Is Transforming the World. Available at: How artificial intelligence is transforming the world | Brookings [accessed March 28, 2024].

www.moe.gov.cn (2023). Deepening Digital Transformation, Building A Bright Future of Education. Available at: Deepening Digital Transformation, Building A Bright Future of Education – Ministry of Education of the People's Republic of China (moe.gov.cn) [accessed March 23, 2024].

PART IV

Impact of Globalization on Entrepreneurship

4 New Trends in Entrepreneurship and the Global Entrepreneurship Index in China, Japan and Bangladesh

Mirjana Radović-Marković

4.1 Introduction

One way of measuring the growth of Chinese companies is through the Fortune Global 500, an annual ranking of the world's top 500 companies by revenue. According to the Fortune Global 500 list for 2022, China has the highest number of companies on the list for the fourth consecutive year, with 145 companies. These 145 Chinese companies on the list contributed 31% of the total revenue of the world's 500 largest corporations, while the 124 US companies in the list accounted for 30% (China.org.cn, 2022). According to Fortune, "aggregate sales for the Fortune Global 500 hit $37.8 trillion, an increase of 19%, which is the highest annual growth rate in the list's history" (SASAC, 2022). Among the world's billion-dollar firms, approximately 900 are from the Greater China region (McKinsey Global Institute, 2020). This latest list confirms China's rising prowess in sectors like manufacturing and infrastructure.

Having grown to significant size at home, Chinese companies are now using M&A to expand their global presence. This strategy began in the resource sector; energy and materials related deals accounted for 62% of outbound M&A between 2006 and 2010. This share fell to 46% between 2011 and 2015, as deals increasingly branched into areas such as technology, real estate, and entertainment. According to Bain & Company (2010), Chinese businesses need to learn several important lessons to replicate the success of companies like ChemChina. One of the lessons is to know which approach works best for them and not assume conventional M&As are their only options.

DOI: 10.4324/9781003602378-8

Table 4.1 Comparison of Top Sectors (2020)

Rank	*USA*	*China*	*Japan*	*Germany*
1.	Financials	Financials	Financials	Automotives
2.	Health care	Energy	Automotives	Financials
3.	Energy	Materials	Technology	Energy
4.	Technology	Wholesalers	Wholesalers	Health care
5.	Retail	Construction	Energy	Transportation

Source: Preparing according to China Power (2021).

According to a research paper by CEIBS (2021), Chinese companies are expanding their global presence by focusing on the domestic market while expanding their presence overseas. The research paper is based on the results of 1,046 participants, and it provides an accurate insight into the efforts of Chinese companies to expand their presence overseas, as well as the opportunities and challenges they face. The research also highlights that Chinese companies are accelerating their efforts to expand overseas. Nearly 14% of companies reported that more than half of their 2020 revenue came from outside China, indicating that Chinese companies are becoming increasingly global (CEIBS, 2021).

More than half of China's top companies participate within three sectors in 2020: finance (21.8%), energy (18.6%), and materials (12.1%). Both in America and Japan, as well as in China, the largest representation of companies is within the financial sector (Table 4.1).

4.2 The Global Entrepreneurship Index (GEI), China, Japan and Bangladesh

The Global Entrepreneurship Index (GEI) is an annual index that measures the health of entrepreneurship ecosystems in 137 countries. It ranks the performance of these countries against each other, providing a picture of how each country performs in both the domestic and international context (GEDI, 2020). The GEI methodology collects data on the entrepreneurial attitudes, abilities, and aspirations of the local population and then weights these against the prevailing social and economic "infrastructure"—this includes aspects such as broadband connectivity and the transport links to external markets.

The Global Entrepreneurship Index (GEI) in China increased from 36.4 in 2015 to 45.9 in 2019, while in Japan it increased from 49.5 in 2015 to 53.3 in 2019. Growth in Japan was more stable and had a linear growth trend. In the same period, the growth of the Global Index of Entrepreneurship in Bangladesh came down from 14.4% in 2015 to 12.5% in 2019 (Table 4.2 and Fig. 4.1). In 2019, the index

Table 4.2 Global Entrepreneurship Index (GEI), 2015–2019

Country	*Year*				
	2015	*2016*	*2017*	*2018*	*2019*
China	36.4	34.9	36.25	41.14	45.9
Japan	49.5	50.6	51.72	51.52	53.3
Bangladesh	14.4	15.2	11.7	11.84	12.5

Source: Preparing according to Knoema (2022).

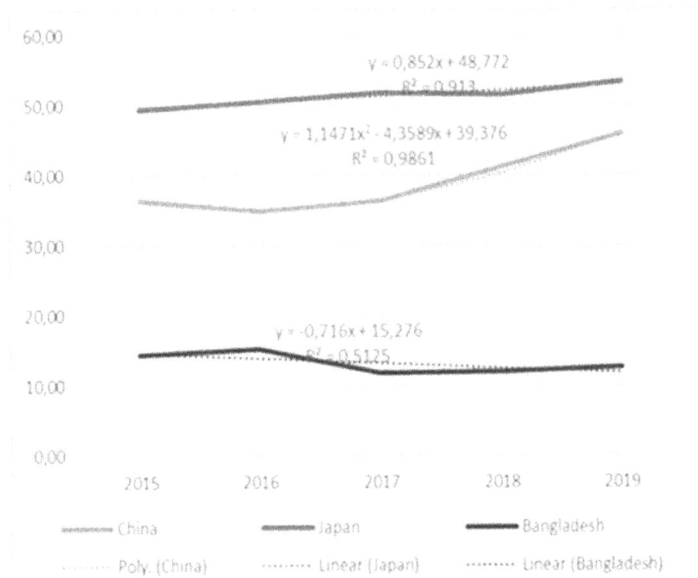

Figure 4.1 Trend of the Global Entrepreneurship Index for China, Japan and Bangladesh.

Source: Author prepared according to data, Knoema (2022).

was 12.5, which is a significant drop from the previous year's index of 13.5. In other words, according to the Global Entrepreneurship Index data, Bangladesh's entrepreneurship index has been decreasing over the past few years (Knoema, 2022). This index has been fluctuating substantially in recent years, but it has been on a downward trend since 2015.

Table 4.2 shows the differences in terms of the achieved Global Index of Entrepreneurship for these countries for the period 2015–2019.

A report by the Business Standard pointed out that entrepreneurship is closely related to economic growth and social transformation. The limitations that came in the way affected the decline of this index in Bangladesh (Momtaz, 2021). These include challenges such as inadequate access to finance, regulatory hurdles, and insufficient infrastructure.

China has been making significant efforts to promote entrepreneurship and innovation in recent years. In line with entrepreneurship promotion, the Chinese government has introduced various policies, including tax breaks, easier registration processes, and public-private investment funds.

In 2016, changes were made in China's national economic strategy (Tse, 2016), which gave impetus to the development of entrepreneurship and investment. Namely, GEI has been growing exponentially since 2016. This turning point is also called "mass entrepreneurship and innovation" as a result of the mentioned changes. The results of the mentioned changes can be seen more significantly already in 2018 and 2019.

Considering that it was necessary to acquire appropriate knowledge for the development of business ideas, especially when the latest technologies began to be introduced to a greater extent in business, young people turn to formal education where they have the opportunity to earn new skills (GEM, 2022/2023, p.42). China has the lowest percentage of adults starting a new business. However, those who do start businesses in China are often at the forefront of using new technologies .This is partly due to the country's strong emphasis on innovation and technological advancement. Namely, according to the Global Entrepreneurship Monitor (GEM) 2022/2023 Global Report, the percentage of adults who are starting or running a new business in China is lower than the average of other economies. The report tracks the percentage of adults who are starting or running a new business, referred to as Total early-stage Entrepreneurial Activity or

TEA. Based on interviews with over 175,000 individuals and experts from 51 economies, the report found that countries have experienced variable impacts from the pandemic. Among the 38 economies that participated in GEM research both in 2019 (prior to the pandemic) and 2022, there were 12 that had a substantially higher level of TEA in 2022 compared to pre-pandemic, and 16 in which TEA levels fell dramatically. In line with this, businesses are almost always generated by the younger generation of entrepreneurs (GEM, 2022/2023).

Regarding the use of new technologies, the Forbes article titled "The One-Person Business Revolution Spreads Around The Globe" (Forbes,2024) states that entrepreneurs in Latin American and the Gulf economies are embracing digital technologies in their small businesses at higher rates than other parts of the world, positioning them for success

4.2.1 Business Environment

A favorable business environment is one of the basic prerequisites for the development of entrepreneurship, the reduction of unemployment and social insecurity, but also the growth of foreign and domestic investments (Radović-Marković & Tomaš, 2019). Namely, the causality between entrepreneurial initiatives and new employment means that when new businesses are started, they often lead to the creation of new jobs (Radović Marković & Tomaš, 2019).

Among the business environment indicators, eleven key ones are mentioned (Table 4.3).

We analyzed the selected countries according to four basic indicators (Table 4. 4).

All these indicators were adopted by China while implementing economic reforms.

Based on the first indicator related to the establishment of companies, Bangladesh had a score of 82.4 in 2020. This score of 82.4 in *Doing Business 2020* indicated that the economy was improving. Of these three countries, for the same year, the best ranked was China with 94.1, followed by Japan with 86.1.

In parallel with reform, the Chinese government also formed working groups that specifically dealt with the improvement of each of these indicators. So far, China has shown the most important progress in terms of obtaining construction permits, introducing electricity, and resolving corporate insolvencies. Further, China implemented a series of measures from 2018 to 2020, which simplified corporate

Table 4.3 Indicators of the Business Environment

Indicators
Establishment of a company
Obtaining building permits
Connection to the electrical network
Property registration
Getting a loan
Protection of minority investors
Paying taxes
Trading across borders
Time and costs for export
Solving insolvency
Labor market regulation

Source: Prepared according to World Bank (2020).

Table 4.4 Countries According to Four Basic Indicators

	Star. Bus.	*Con. Per.*	*Getting El.*	*Reg. Property*
Bangladesh	82.40	61.10	34.90	29.00
China	94.10	77.30	95.40	81.00
Japan	86.10	83.10	93.20	75.60

Source: Preparing according to World Bank (2020).

income tax, labor taxes, value added tax declarations, and e-delivery of invoices (Doing Business, 2020, p.51). China has also introduced major facilitations in cross-border trade.

Bangladesh reduced costs for starting a business and thus supported potential entrepreneurs in establishing their companies.

Bangladesh also accelerated the acquisition of electricity. In recent years, investments in the digitization of business and in the training of employees in companies have been increasing. This is how business is modernized.

Although Japan is one of the most significant large countries in the world (third in terms of GDP), it has a lot of restrictions in terms of establishing a business. First of all, it is a complicated procedure with a complicated and large bureaucracy. Japan ranks 43rd in the world for the time it takes to register a property, based on the World Bank Doing Business 2020 report, taking 13 days, with six procedures to be followed.

According to the World Bank's Doing Business 2023 report, China, Japan, and Bangladesh are ranked as follows in terms of ease of Doing business (World Bank, 2023):

1. China: Ranked 31st out of 190 economies surveyed, with a score of 77.9 out of 100.
2. Japan: Ranked 30th out of 190 economies surveyed, with a score of 78.0 out of 100.
3. Bangladesh: Ranked 168th out of 190 economies surveyed, with a score of 53.8 out of 100.

The data shows that China and Japan were almost equally ranked, that is 30th the place was occupied by Japan and right behind it was China, while for the same year 2020, Bangladesh was at the back and noticeably lagging behind these two countries in 168th position out of 190 countries

The integration of selected countries into international economic flows often leads to enhanced entrepreneurial activities, due to several factors displayed in Figures 4.2, 4.3, and 4.4.

Comparing the global index of entrepreneurship and the index of globalization, our analysis showed a strong correlation between the

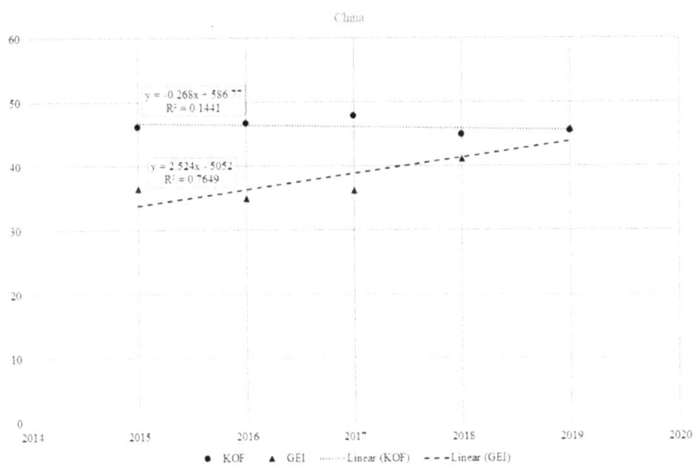

Figure 4.2 Development of entrepreneurship in China (2015–2019).

Source: Author.

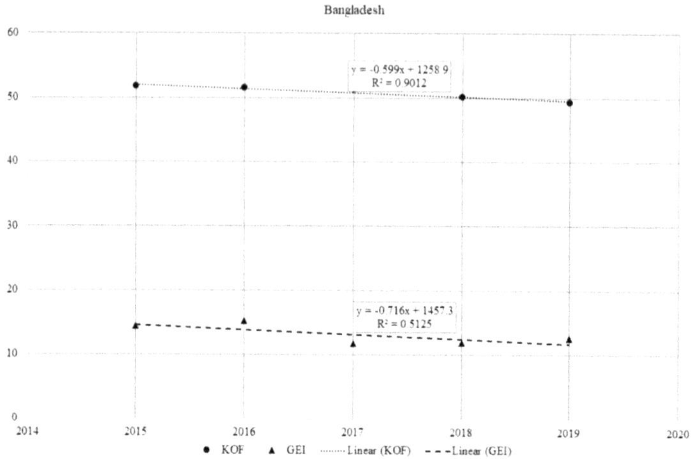

Figure 4.3 Development of entrepreneurship in Bangladesh (2015–2019).

Source: Author.

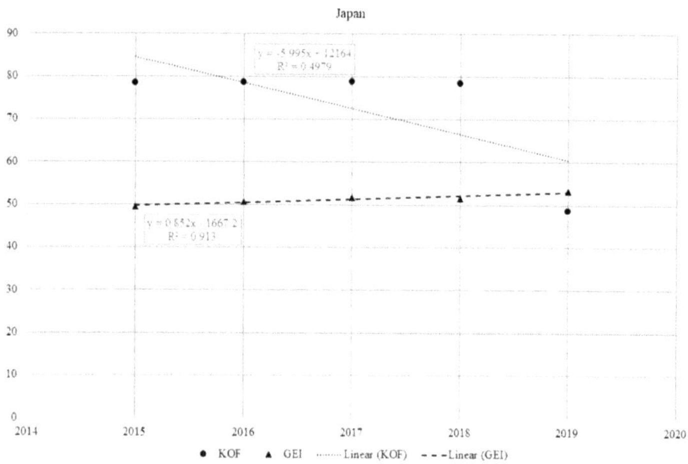

Figure 4.4 Development of entrepreneurship in Japan (2015–2019).

Source: Author.

level of globalization and the level of entrepreneurship for China, i.e. correlation is R^2 =0.7683; a correlation greater than 0.75 is considered to be a "strong" correlation between two variables, GEI and KOF. Namely, our study shows that globalization has had a significant impact on entrepreneurship in China in recent years. The country's economic transition since the 1980s has greatly unleashed entrepreneurship and private enterprise development (Canfei, Jiangyong, and Haifeng, 2019). The Chinese government has recognized entrepreneurship as one of the key driving forces of sustained economic development and is accordingly making many efforts to encourage and facilitate entrepreneurial activity. It has helped China achieve rapid economic growth and poverty reduction. China's share of world trade has also increased significantly, from less than 1% in 1978 to over 14% in 2022 (WTO, 2023). According to World Trade Statistical Review (WTO, 2023), China increased its exports the most, recording over 30% of cars sold globally (the largest exporter of automotive products in 2022).

When it comes to the impact of globalization on entrepreneurship in Bangladesh, our research has shown that this impact is moderate. Globalization also has played a significant role in the growth of the Japanese economy. Japan has achieved economic growth by accelerating "external" globalization through the development of trade deals and direct foreign investment (FDI) (Urata,2022). The globalization of the Japanese economy is characterized by close relationships through production networks with rapidly growing Asian countries. In this context, by correlating the globalization index and the global entrepreneurship index in Japan, a strong influence can be observed, as in the case of China (R2=0.6051).

4.3 The Entrepreneurial Spirit Index (ESI)

The Entrepreneurial Spirit Index is a metric that measures the level of entrepreneurial spirit in a given population (Terry, 2023). It is a composite index that takes into account various factors such as the number of new businesses created, the number of patents filed, and the level of education and training in entrepreneurship. The index is used to identify areas where entrepreneurship is thriving and to develop policies that promote entrepreneurship.

IPSOS research showed that one third of the population or 37% citizens globally have "very high" entrepreneurial spirit (IPSOS, 2021).

According to a 2021 survey by IPSOS, the entrepreneurial spirit index for Japan is low, with only 17% of respondents having a high or very high entrepreneurial spirit, while 35% of respondents had a low entrepreneurial spirit (IPSOS, 2021). One of the reasons why the entrepreneurial spirit index is low is the lack of venture capitalists who tend to invest in startups elsewhere in the world (BBC, 2015). Another reason is the relative dearth of opportunity-driven entrepreneurship, which has contributed to the nation's economic malaise over the past two decades (Blind, 2015). In addition, it was identified that decreased interest in starting entrepreneurial firms due to the fear of taking on high business risks, as well as the fear of unemployment have a significant negative impact on the entrepreneurial spirit in Japan.

There are several ways Japan can improve its entrepreneurial spirit. One way is to encourage more venture capitalists to invest in startups in Japan. This can be done by creating tax incentives for venture capitalists and by making it easier for foreign venture capitalists to invest in Japanese startups (Tobin, 2015). Another way is to promote opportunity-driven entrepreneurship by creating an environment that encourages innovation and creativity. This can be done by providing more funding for research and development, by creating more incubators and accelerators for startups, and by providing more support for entrepreneurs. Finally, Japan can improve its entrepreneurial spirit by changing the business culture to be more accepting of risk-taking and failure. This can be done by promoting a culture of innovation and creativity, and by providing more education and training in entrepreneurship,

The entrepreneurial spirit index distribution in China as of September 2018 was such that 48% of respondents ranked as having a very high entrepreneurial spirit (Textor, 2021). The Chinese government places a high value on the positive role entrepreneurs and the entrepreneurial spirit play in economic development and social progress. Fostering the entrepreneurial spirit can provide further protection and motivation.

For Bangladesh, we do not have data related to the entrepreneurship index and accordingly could not compare it with the other two large selected countries. However, it is known that Bangladesh has a low level of entrepreneurial activity compared to other countries in the region. However, there are several initiatives underway to promote entrepreneurship in the country. One such initiative is the Get in the Ring (GITR) competition, which is a global startup competition that aims to recognize the role of startups and startup tools as models for creativity and innovation (Mostafiz, 2021).

The importance of fostering an entrepreneurial spirit can certainly contribute to the launch of new businesses and the realization of entrepreneurial ideas in the future. Global research has shown that those who have a much higher level of entrepreneurial spirit (64%) are more likely to start their own business than those who do not have it or have it to a lesser extent (19% entrepreneurial spirit) (IPSOS, 2021).

4.4 Conclusion

Over the years, the number of entrepreneurs in China has grown, which is also the case with the other countries that we have taken into consideration. Entrepreneurs are characterized by different business ideas, different business ambitions, as well as the diversity of their backgrounds and knowledge. What they have in common, regardless of their differences, is a great curiosity and desire for success.

Japan has been making efforts to create innovation ecosystems, including the formation of centers of innovation that can be expanded on a global basis based on the Strategy for the Creation of Startup Ecosystems, as well as support for J-Startup, a program for nurturing global startups. Innovation ecosystems are characterized by the presence of a variety of actors, including entrepreneurs, investors, universities, research institutions, and large corporations, who work together to create and commercialize new products and services (JETRO Global Connection, 2020). Therefore, it is reasonable to conclude that globalization has facilitated technology entrepreneurship in Japan by fostering the rise of innovation ecosystems (Mulas et al., 2021).

Globalization has had a significant impact on entrepreneurship development in Bangladesh. The country's economy grew rapidly during the 1990s as it liberalized its markets and became increasingly integrated into the world economy. This improved performance owed itself both to a slowdown in population growth and a sustained increase in the rate of GDP growth, which averaged 5.2% annually during the second half of the 1990s (Wahiduddin, 2003). However, the global recession of 2001 hit Bangladesh hard and left behind the economic momentum of the 1990s. After this recession, and especially after the damage and distress caused by the COVID 19 pandemic, entrepreneurs in Bangladesh began to explore new opportunities for a "global reset." In line with this, a 2021 report by Future Startup suggests that Bangladesh's startup scene has grown rapidly in recent years, producing increasing numbers of high-quality startups (Kader, 2023).

The report highlights that the country's entrepreneurs face several challenges, including inadequate access to finance, lack of infrastructure, and limited access to technology and information. However, the report also suggests that the country's startup ecosystem is evolving, and the future looks promising. Namely, Bangladesh's economy is growing rapidly, and its startup ecosystem is evolving. The country's entrepreneurs face several challenges, but the future looks promising. A multi-stakeholder effort across the ecosystem, from the implementation of policies and legal frameworks to the development of human capital and entrepreneurship culture and strengthening access to finance, support services, digital and technological solutions, and infrastructure, is required to catalyze the potential of youth entrepreneurship.

Finally, it should be recalled that the global environment, as already mentioned, significantly changes standard business and entrepreneurial practices. Today, completely new forms of entrepreneurial activities are emerging. Also, some previously existing forms of activity acquire new content and are increasingly important.

Finally, it can be concluded that the analysis of the quality of entrepreneurship through the global entrepreneurship index should indicate what actions are necessary to be undertaken in order to indicate the needs of entrepreneurs and the gaps in the entrepreneurial ecosystem.

Compared to Japan and Bangladesh, China achieved the greatest economic improvement (Doing Business, 2020). However, at the global level, in addition to China, the countries that achieved improvements are also Saudi Arabia, Jordan, Togo, Bahrain, Tajikistan, Pakistan, and Kuwait.

References

Bain & Company (2010). Growing beyond China: Five Things Chinese Companies Need to Know about Global Expansion. Available at: Growing beyond China: Five things Chinese companies need to know about global expansion | Bain & Company [accessed April 12, 2024].

BBC (2015). Where Are Japan's Entrepreneurs?. Available at: Why are there so few Japanese entrepreneurs? – BBC News [accessed April 12, 2024].

Blind, G.D. (2015). *Investigating Entrepreneurial Spirit with the Rule Approach: Why Self-employment Is on the Decline in Japan*. Cham, Switzerland: Springer.

Canfei, H., Jiangyong, L., and Haifeng, Q. (2019). Entrepreneurship in China. *Small Business Economics*, Vol. 52, No. 3, Special Issue: Entrepreneurship in China (March 2019), pp. 563–572.

CEIBS (2021). How Are Chinese Companies Going Global? Available at: How are Chinese companies going global? | CEIBS [accessed Apr 16 2024].

China.org.cn (2022). Chinese Companies Top List of Fortune 500. Available at: Chinese companies top list of Fortune 500 – China.org.cn [accessed April 06, 2024].

China Power (2021). How Dominant are Chinese Companies Globally? Available at: https://chinapower.csis.org/chinese-companies-global-500 [accessed April 05, 2024].

Global Entrepreneurship and Development Institute (GEDI) (2020). Global Entrepreneurship Index. Available at: Entrepreneurship & Business Statistics | GEDI

Global Entrepreneurship Monitor (GEM) (2022/2023). Global Report Adapting to A "New Normal". Available at: GEM Global Entrepreneurship Monitor.

Global Entrepreneurship Monitor (GEM) (2022). New Gem South Africa National Report: Early-Stage Entrepreneurs Are Growing Into Established Businesses. Available at: Entrepreneurial spirit index by country 2021 | Statista [accessed April 05, 2024].

IPSOS (2021). Entrepreneurial Spirit. Available at: Global Entrepreneurialism 2021 (ipsos.com) [accessed April 10, 2024].

JETRO Global Connection (2020). About Japan's Innovation Ecosystem. Available at: About Japan's Innovation Ecosystem | Reports – JETRO Global Connection – Japan External Trade Organization – JETRO [accessed April 22, 2024].

Kader, R. (2022). Bangladesh Startup Funding Report 2021. Available at: Bangladesh Startup Funding Report 2021 – Future Startup [accessed April 22, 2024].

Knoema (2022). China – Global entrepreneurship index. Available at: China Global entrepreneurship index, 2015–2022 – knoema.com [accessed April 22, 2024].

McKinsey Global Institute (2020). Digital Globalization: The New Era of Global Flows. Available at: Digital globalization: The new era of global flows | McKinsey [accessed April 22, 2024].

Momtaz, U.A. (2021). Unleashing Entrepreneurship Growth in Bangladesh: Why and How. Available at: Unleashing entrepreneurship growth in Bangladesh: Why and how | The Business Standard (tbsnews.net) [accessed April 12, 2024].

Mostafiz, O. (2021). Fostering Entrepreneurship in Bangladesh. Available at: Entrepreneurship & Startups: Fostering Entrepreneurship in Bangladesh (freiheit.org) [accessed April 02, 2024].

Mulas, V., Astudillo, P., Riku, T., Wyne, J., and Zhang, X. (2021). *Tokyo Start-Up Ecosystem*. Tokyo: World Bank.

Radović Marković, M., and Tomas, R. (2019). *Globalisation Impact on Entrepreneurship in Small Countries*. Abingdon, Oxon; New York: Routledge, 189 p.

SASAC (2022). Chinese Companies Top List of Fortune 500. Available at: Chinese Companies Top List of Fortune 500 (sasac.gov.cn) [accessed April 06, 2024].

Terry, S. (2023). Fuel Your Entrepreneurial Spirit with These 4 Tips. Available at: Fuel Your Entrepreneurial Spirit With These 4 Tips (leaders.com) [accessed April 03, 2024].

Textor, C. (2021). Entrepreneurial Spirit Index Distribution in China 2018. Available at: China: entrepreneurial spirit index distribution 2018 | Statista [accessed June 06, 2023].

Tobin, R. (2015). Encouraging Entrepreneurial Spirit in Japan. Available at: Encouraging Entrepreneurial Spirit in Japan – Deutsches Institut für Japanstudien (dijtokyo.org); DIJ-Forum_150611.pdf [accessed April 06, 2024].

Tse, E. (2016). The Rise of Entrepreneurship in China. *Forbes*. Available at: The Rise of Entrepreneurship in China (forbes.com) [accessed June 06, 2023].

Urata, S. (2022). Globalization of Japanese Economy: Reality and Impacts. Available at: Globalization of Japanese Economy: Reality and Impacts – WORLD INSIGHT [accessed June 06, 2023].

Wahiduddin, M. (2003). Bangladesh Faces the Challenge of Globalization. Available at: Bangladesh Faces the Challenge of Globalization | YaleGlobal Online [accessed June 16, 2023].

World Bank (2020). Comparing Business Regulation in 190 Economies. Available at: Doing Business 2020 (worldbank.org) [accessed April 02, 2024].

World Bank (2023). Ease of Doing Business Index by Country 2023. Available at: Ease of Doing Business Index by Country 2024 (worldpopulationreview.com) [accessed June 10, 2023].

WTO (2023). World Trade Statistical Review 2023. Available at: World Trade Statistical Review 2023 (wto.org) [accessed April 02, 2024].

5 Entrepreneurial Environment and Small and Medium Enterprises in China

Yao Ouyang

The entrepreneurial environment is a collection of various factors related to entrepreneurial activities, including macro and micro environments. On a macro level, it represents the sum of societal factors that bring market opportunities to businesses, including political, economic, social, technological, legal, and natural factors. On a micro level, it includes the various factors that directly impact business operations, such as customers, competitors, marketing channels, and public relations. The entrepreneurial environment consists of an integrated system of macro and micro environments, influencing a country or region's entrepreneurial vitality and performance.

5.1 Entrepreneurial Environment, Business Environment and Degree of Openness

5.1.1 Entrepreneurial Environment and Business Environment

The most important aspect for entrepreneurs is the business environment. In 2001, the World Bank introduced an index system for assessing the development environment of the private sector in various countries. The system evaluates the business environment of different economies based on five indicators: starting a business, obtaining financing, hiring employees, executing contracts, and processing bankruptcy. This system has been continuously improved and has become an important indicator of particular interest to some countries' governments and policymakers (Table 5.1).

Since joining the World Trade Organization in 2001, the Chinese government has been dedicated to improving the business environment.

DOI: 10.4324/9781003602378-9

Table 5.1 World Bank "Doing Business 2020 Report" Evaluation

Indicators	*Evaluation System Evaluation Content*
Starting a Business	Procedures, time, cost, minimum paid-in capital requirement
Dealing with Construction Permits	Steps, time, cost, building quality control index
Getting Electricity	Steps, days/time, cost of getting electricity connection, reliability of supply, and transparency of tariffs index
Registering Property	Steps, time, cost for property transfer, land administration quality index
Getting Credit	Credit and information records for movable collateral
Protecting Minority	Investors range of disclosure index, extent of director liability, ease of shareholder suits index, range of shareholder rights index, extent of ownership and control index
Paying Taxes	All tax regulations applicable to the firm and post-filing processes in terms of payments, time, total tax, and contribution rate
Trading Across Borders	Time and cost to export a product with comparative advantage and import auto parts
Enforcing Contracts	Time, cost, number of procedures index
Resolving Insolvency	Time, cost, recovery rate index, strength of insolvency framework index
Labor Market Regulation	Employment, working hours, layoffs, job quality
Government Procurement	Procedures and time required for participation and obtaining public procurement contracts, regulatory framework of public procurement

Sources: Compiled from World Bank 《Doing Business 2020》, https://documents1.worldbank.org/curated/en/688761571934946384/pdf/Doing-Business-2020-Comparing-Business-Regulation-in-190-Economies.pdf

It has created favorable conditions for all market entities to invest and start businesses, leading to continuous enhancements in the entrepreneurial climate for companies. According to the World Bank's Doing Business report data, China's overall ranking in the business environment has rapidly improved, climbing from 96th in 2013 to 31st in 2022 (Table 5.2).

In July 2020, the World Bank released a special report titled "China's Success in Optimizing the Business Environment: Drivers

Table 5.2 China's Global Business Environment Overall Ranking Over the Past 10 Years

Year	*Ranking*
2013	96
2014	96
2015	90
2016	84
2017	78
2018	78
2019	46
2020	31
2021	31
2022	31

Sources: Compiled from World Bank (Doing Business 2020), https://documents1.worldbank.org/curated/en/688761571934946384/pdf/Doing-Business-2020-Comparing-Business-Regulation-in-190-Economies.pdf

of Reform and Future Opportunities for Reform," which posited that China's business environment had seen unprecedented improvement over the past few years, placing it among the top 10 economies with the fastest reform pace in the last two years. "Over the past decade, China has reformed indicators across all areas covered by the Doing Business reports, leaving us with a profound impression. Thanks to vigorous reforms in the business environment, China is recognized as the most important reformer among large economies and has become one of the top ten fastest-growing economies in the world." The World Bank report also specifically analyzed the reasons behind China's successful reforms, identifying six main driving factors: (1) high-level leadership attention to the reform agenda; (2) local policy experimentation; (3) domestic and international knowledge exchange; (4) robust implementation and accountability for reform agendas; (5) active participation of the private sector; and (6) widespread application of e-government services. Cities like Shanghai exemplify this, where business environment reforms have become one of the main factors influencing economic growth. In recent years, Shanghai has gained a competitive edge in the fierce global competition with cities like Tokyo, Seoul, Singapore, and San Francisco.

The Chinese government has long been committed to improving the business environment for enterprises, optimizing the institutional elements and social conditions involved in market economy activities to attract more talent, capital, and technology for innovation and entrepreneurship. In 2019, the State Council issued the "Regulations on Optimizing the Business Environment," whose main contents include: (1) Protection of market entities. Market entities have the right to operate independently according to law, with equal access to capital, technology, human resources, land ownership, and natural resources. At the same time, the state protects their property rights and intellectual property rights. (2) Market environment. The country continues to relax market access, implements a nationwide unified negative list system for market access, and strengthens the construction of the social

Table 5.3 Top 50 Cities for Business Environment in China, 2023

No.	*City*	*Index*	*No.*	*City*	*Index*
1	Shanghai	1	26	Xi'an	0.774
2	Beijing	0.986	27	Nanchang	0.765
3	Shenzhen	0.975	28	Zhengzhou	0.754
4	Hangzhou	0.954	29	Taiyuan	0.738
5	Suzhou	0.952	30	Kunming	0.731
6	Hefei	0.95	31	Yantai	0.719
7	Guangzhou	0.942	32	Guiyang	0.712
8	Ningbo	0.928	33	Changchun	0.709
9	Nanjing	0.917	34	Harbin	0.706
10	Changsha	0.901	35	Shaoxing	0.698
11	Wuhan	0.9	36	Nantong	0.686
12	Xiamen	0.889	37	Quanzhou	0.678
13	Chengdu	0.878	38	Shijiazhuang	0.669
14	Chongqing	0.873	39	Wuhu	0.664
15	Wuxi	0.871	40	Nanning	0.662
16	Qingdao	0.868	41	Zhongshan	0.656
17	Changzhou	0.856	42	Wenzhou	0.643
18	Tianjin	0.851	43	Chuzhou	0.638
19	Foshan	0.832	44	Weifang	0.636
20	Dongguan	0.828	45	Yancheng	0.635
21	Jinan	0.809	46	Huizhou	0.629
22	Fuzhou	0.794	47	Lu'an	0.626
23	Dalian	0.791	48	Urumqi	0.624
24	Zhuhai	0.788	49	Hohhot	0.619
25	Shenyang	0.784	50	Xuzhou	0.606

Sources: Compiled from Peking University & Wuhan University (Evaluation of Doing Business in Chinese Cities 2023). https://opendata.pku.edu.cn/dataset.xhtml?persistentId=doi:10.18170/DVN/9NJDWE

credit system. (3) Government services. Government departments provide standardized, comprehensive, and efficient administrative services to market entities, establishing convenient and unobstructed channels for handling complaints and reports concerning the business environment. (4) Regulatory enforcement. A cross-regional administrative law enforcement linkage response and collaboration mechanism are implemented. (5) Legal safeguards. Administrative regulations, rules, and normative documents related to the activities of market production and operation entities are formulated to provide market entities with efficient and convenient dispute-resolution methods. To ensure the implementation of these regulations, the General Office of the State Council issued the "Opinions on Further Optimizing the Business Environment to Better Serve Market Entities" in 2020 and the "Opinions on Further Optimizing the Business Environment and Reducing the Systemic Transaction Costs of Market Entities" in 2022, thus promoting the optimization of the business environment nationwide (Table 5.3).

5.1.2 China's Domestic and International Openness

The Chinese government has consistently pushed for domestic and international openness to foster a favorable entrepreneurial and business environment. Domestic openness primarily aims to break down the barriers between different regions within the country, allowing entrepreneurs to freely enter and exit various regions, thus creating a vast space for entrepreneurship and market opportunities.

China is a vast country with a land area of 9.6 million square kilometers and consists of 34 provincial-level administrative units, including 23 provinces, five autonomous regions, four municipalities directly under the central government, and two special administrative regions. Such an ample space has the potential to form a massive market scope. However, suppose regions within the country are not open to each other, and institutional barriers are artificially set up. In that case, it leads to independent and isolated regional spaces, resulting in smaller market sizes. In recent years, observers have found that the domestic market suffers from severe regional segmentation, with local protectionism prevalent and some artificially set barriers hindering market entities' entry and exit. This situation has led to unequal opportunities for entrepreneurs and barriers to the flow of goods and production factors, causing obstructions and inefficiencies in circulation.

To address these issues, the central government formulated the "Opinions on Accelerating the Construction of a National Unified Market" in March 2022, proposing six policy measures:

(1) Ensuring uniformity of fundamental market institutional rules, including unified systems for property rights protection, market access, fair competition, and social credit.
(2) Advancing the high-standard interconnectivity of market infrastructure, including building modern circulation networks, improving market information exchange channels, and optimizing market transaction platforms.
(3) Constructing unified factor markets and resource markets, including improving land, labor, and capital markets and accelerating the establishment of energy and carbon emission markets and water rights trading markets.
(4) Building a unified commodity and service market, including improving the goods quality system, standards, and measurement systems and enhancing the quality of consumer services.
(5) Establishing a fair and unified market regulatory system, including improving uniform market supervision rules, uniform law enforcement procedures, and high-level regulatory services.
(6) Preventing market monopolies and unfair competition, including preventing the abuse of administrative powers, eliminating restrictions on market competition, breaking down local protectionism and regional barriers, and addressing regulations that hinder legal equal access and exit.

Although a rising power like China possesses a vast domestic market, it still needs the larger scale of the international market for several reasons: first, to expand the scope of the domestic market; second, to elevate the level of the domestic market through access to high-quality international markets; and third, to introduce global quality factors and resources. Therefore, the Chinese government has made opening up to the international economy a basic national policy, persistently promoting international openness over the long term.

In recent years, the focus of China's openness has shifted towards institutional openness. In 2018, in response to new circumstances, the Chinese government pushed for comprehensive international openness, transitioning from openness based on the flow of goods and factors to one based on rules and other institutional factors,

Table 5.4 2019 Openness Level Ranking of China, Japan, and Other Countries/Regions

Degree of Domestic Openness			*Degree of International Openness*		
Ranking	*Countries*	*Score*	*Ranking*	*Countries*	*Score*
1	Hong Kong, China	9.06	1	Austria	9.08
2	Netherlands	8.79	2	Hong Kong, China	9.06
3	Singapore	8.62	4	Sweden	8.89
6	Germany	8.47	8	United Kingdom	8.54
7	United States	8.43	10	United States	7.66
19	France	7.38	29	France	7.16
34	Japan	6.78	45	Japan	6.00
38	Mainland China	4.68	59	Mainland China	5.27

Sources: Compiled from Institute of World Economics and Politics, Chinese Academy of Social Sciences & Research Center of Hongqiao International Economic Forum (Open World Report 2023), www.iwep.org.cn/cbw/cbw_ndfxbg/ndfxbg_sjkfbg/sjkfbg_cbyfb/202401/t20240124_5730574.shtml

including regulations, management practices, and standards. To advance institutional openness, the government has accelerated the establishment of free trade zones, with zones now established in Shanghai, Guangdong, Tianjin, Fujian, Liaoning, Zhejiang, Henan, Hubei, Chongqing, Sichuan, Shaanxi, and other provinces and cities, forming an integrated pattern of openness. Additionally, the "Regional Comprehensive Economic Partnership" (RCEP) that China joined officially took effect in January 2022, marking a significant expansion of China's economic openness and showcasing new development opportunities and prospects (Table 5.4).

5.2 SME (Small and Medium-sized Enterprise) Policy Support System and Environmental Analysis

British development economist E.F. Schumacher (1911–1977), in his work "Small is Beautiful," proposed the advantages of small scale, which include: (1) small companies have their advantages, such as flexibility, simpler internal management compared to large companies, and the ease with which employees can unite; (2) developed countries have the prerequisites for large-scale production, whereas developing countries should opt for "intermediate technology" for mass production to enhance the productivity of human hands and brains; and (3) the production by large-scale companies leads to a decrease in efficiency, causing environmental pollution and resource depletion, and undermining human happiness.

In China's reform and opening up, SMEs, as an essential economic entity of the market economy, have seen their status and role in the national economy increasingly elevated. Entering the 21st century, the Chinese government particularly emphasized developing SMEs. Since 2001, the growth rates of various indicators for Chinese SMEs have been higher than those of large enterprises. In 2006, SMEs accounted for 99.3% of the total enterprises in China, contributing 55.6% to the GDP, 86.2% of tax revenue, 62.3% of exports, and 75% of urban employment. Clearly, SMEs have become an important engine for the socio-economic development of China. However, the development of SMEs also faces some challenges: Firstly, the management of these enterprises is relatively extensive and needs more sophisticated management experience; Secondly, they engage in low-cost competition strategies, resulting in low-profit margins. More importantly, the development environment for SMEs is suboptimal, with many barriers to market entry and difficulties in financing.

5.2.1 Reform Framework of the "Promotion Law for Small and Medium Enterprises"

To improve the entrepreneurial environment for SMEs, in June 2002, the Standing Committee of the National People's Congress passed the "Promotion Law for Small and Medium Enterprises of the People's Republic of China," proposing a policy framework to support the development of SMEs.

(1) Policies to protect the legal rights and interests of SMEs. For example, no unit or individual may infringe on the property and other legal rights and interests of SMEs; no unit may charge fees, impose fines, or allocate financial burdens to SMEs in violation of laws and regulations; and the right of SMEs to fair competition and fair trade according to law is protected.

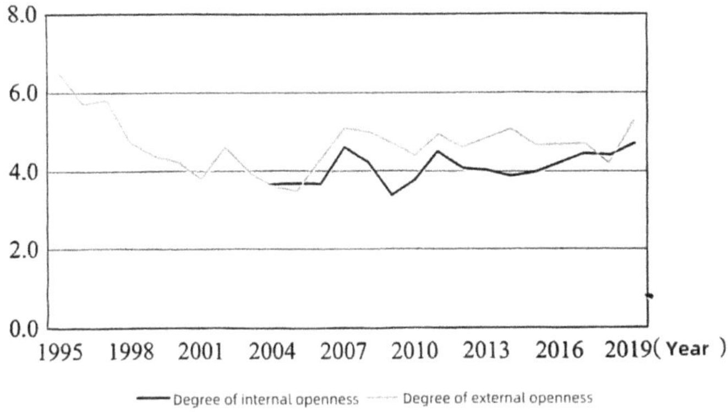

Figure 5.1 Changes in the Degree of Openness in Mainland China (1995–2022).

Sources: Compiled from IMD (World Competitiveness Yearbook), www.imd.org/centers/wcc/world-competitiveness-center/rankings/world-competitiveness-ranking/

(2) Fiscal and financial policies to promote the development of SMEs. For example, establish SME categories in fiscal budgets and arrange special funds to support the development of SMEs; encourage commercial banks and credit cooperatives to increase credit support for SMEs by adjusting credit structures; encourage state policy financial institutions to provide financial services to SMEs in various forms.
(3) Policies to encourage entrepreneurship and innovation among SMEs. For example, simplifying the registration procedures for establishing SMEs and providing support in areas such as planning and land use; establishing various technical service institutions, enabling technology innovation projects to enjoy loan interest subsidy policies; encouraging social intermediary organizations to provide entrepreneurship guidance, enterprise diagnosis, and information consulting services to SMEs.

With the introduction of the "SME Law," both central and local governments have increased financial support for SMEs, subsequently establishing several special funds and foundations aimed at supporting

SMEs: (1) Special Funds for SME Development, mainly supporting the construction of the SME service system as well as entrepreneurship and technological innovation. (2) SME Development Fund, mainly used for entrepreneurship guidance, talent training, and construction of credit guarantee systems for SMEs. (3) Technology Innovation Fund for SMEs, mainly used for loan interest subsidies, grants, and funding for emerging industry projects of technology-oriented SMEs. (4) Special Subsidy Funds for SME Service Systems, mainly used for subsidizing SME service institutions to carry out entrepreneurship, training, and credit services. (5) International Market Development Funds for SMEs, enabling SMEs to participate in overseas exhibitions, quality management system certification, overseas bidding, and developing new markets.

5.2.2 SME Development Environment and Its Assessment

After introducing the "Promotion Law for Small and Medium Enterprises," governments at all levels formulated corresponding policy measures to support the development of SMEs, continuously improving the SME development environment. In 2022, the China SME Development Promotion Center conducted a third-party assessment of the SME development environment, selecting four municipalities, five cities designated in the state plan, and 27 provincial capitals for evaluation. Data were collected through reports from local government departments, online surveys of enterprises, field investigations, public statistical data, and government websites; meanwhile, a multi-dimensional assessment system was built to evaluate and analyze the trend of improvement and new issues in the SME environment. The assessment results exhibited the following features:

(1) A fair competition market and legal environment were created through deepening reforms. Measures such as "barrier-free approvals" and "non-intrusive supervision" were implemented, achieving lower thresholds, streamlined processes, and cost savings; in government procurement, electronic tendering was promoted, and the management of bid bonds was standardized to ensure fair participation of micro and small enterprises in competition; particular attention was given to the construction of a legal business environment, building an integrated coordination

mechanism, smoothing channels for enterprise complaints, and providing "one-stop" rights protection services.

(2) An inclusive financial ecosystem was built through credit structure adjustment. By establishing SME risk compensation funds, broader financial resources were guided to serve the real economy, and financial institutions were encouraged to optimize internal resource allocation and policy arrangements. By the end of 2021, the balance of inclusive small and micro-business loans increased by 25% year-over-year, and the average interest rate of newly issued loans decreased by 0.2 percentage points from the previous year. Survey results showed that 40.23% of businesses were very satisfied with the financing environment, and 43.89% were satisfied.

(3) A new technology industrialization ecosystem was established by optimizing pathways. Relying on high-tech industrial research institutes and SME innovation development funds, a superior small business incubation system was built to promote the rapid implementation of high-quality invention patents; through the combination of industry, education, and research, a complete chain of collaborative innovation was constructed, creating an ecosystem where large, medium, and small enterprises integrate innovation; leading enterprises in the innovation and industrial chains drove SME technological innovation, aiming to develop critical components to strengthen and supplement the chains.

(4) Various preferential policies were ensured to be implemented efficiently through service optimization. SME "group services" and "cloud services" platforms were built, integrating high-quality resources to provide "one-stop" services to small and micro enterprises; a convenient and efficient "express channel" for preferential policies was created to achieve comprehensive acceptance and precise delivery of preferential items; a digital tax payment platform was developed, constantly innovating ways to serve businesses, enhancing the efficiency of data sharing and governance, and precisely implementing various tax preferential policies.

5.3 New Trends in SME Development

Chinese SMEs, the largest and most dynamic group of enterprises, have become the leading force in national economic development. The number of SMEs has rapidly expanded, with over 52 million by the end of 2022, marking a 51% increase from 2018; an average of 23,800 new enterprises were established daily in 2022, 1.3 times the number in 2018. Meanwhile, the quality of SMEs has continuously improved, giving rise to a batch of high-tech and highly efficient quality enterprises and cultivating a group of specialized and sophisticated "little giant" enterprises. Statistically, SMEs account for 90% of all enterprises nationwide, providing 80% of urban labor force jobs, 50% of tax revenue, 60% of GDP, and 70% of technological innovation achievements. SMEs have adopted new organizational structures and technological means in their development, thus exhibiting new characteristics and trends.

5.3.1 The Emergence of Specialized and Sophisticated SMEs

The Chinese government has introduced the concept of specialized and sophisticated SMEs, referring to those with "specialization, refinement, uniqueness, and innovation" as their four major advantages. These SMEs often focus on specific niche markets, possessing unique technologies, processes, or formulas, and can produce specialized products with local characteristics or special functions. They emphasize refined management in their production processes and develop and produce high-tech products with independent intellectual property rights through careful design and technological innovation. Specialized and sophisticated SMEs represent the excellence within China's SME community and have become a crucial support for building a manufacturing powerhouse.

5.3.1.1 Specific Standards for Specialized and Sophisticated SMEs Include:

(1) Specialization: Deeply cultivating core businesses
   ① Identifying niche areas and targeting specific goals.
   ② Concentrating efforts to deepen expertise and determine core business directions.
   ③ Establishing specialized collaboration systems with leading enterprises.
(2) Refinement: Pursuing excellence
   ① Engaging in long-term refined R&D to design and manufacture high-quality products.
   ② Building independent brands and creating excellent quality.
   ③ Achieving high recognition and reputation.

(3) Uniqueness: Exclusive skills
   ① Establishing differential positioning to create unique products.
   ② Operating in small units to provide comprehensive support on a small scale.
   ③ Leading product iteration development with trend-setting.
(4) Innovation: Technological innovation
   ① Seeking advantages in original innovation.
   ② Acquiring high-value patents through innovation.
   ③ Achieving commercial application and industrial breakthroughs.

In recent years, national and local governments have introduced policy measures to guide SMEs towards a specialized and sophisticated development path. The specific policy tools have become more systematic, forming a full-cycle and comprehensive support system.

Full-cycle support: A complete, life-cycle cultivation system entails incubating and nurturing outstanding SMEs and promoting their development into single-item champions and leading enterprises.

Comprehensive support: Includes not only traditional SME support policies but also specially formulated policies for precise support of specialized and sophisticated SMEs, including fiscal and tax policies, financing policies, innovation policies, and optimization of the entrepreneurial environment.

The Chinese government has set the goal of gradient cultivation of SMEs: The first tier is to cultivate a vast number of innovative SMEs; the second tier is to cultivate specialized and sophisticated SMEs; the third tier is to cultivate specialized and sophisticated "little giant" enterprises; the fourth tier is to cultivate single-item champion enterprises in manufacturing. Since 2019, the Ministry of Industry and Information Technology has cultivated 8,997 specialized and sophisticated "little giant" enterprises; by the end of 2021, these enterprises achieved an annual operating income of 3.7 trillion yuan, with a total annual profit of over 380 billion yuan, and a profit margin over 10%. Among them, 21% had an annual revenue of less than 100 million yuan, 74% had annual revenue between 100 million and 1 billion yuan, and the remaining 400 enterprises exceeded 1 billion yuan in annual revenue

5.3.2 "Specialized and Sophisticated 'Little Giants'" Enterprise Examples

Depam Pump Technology Co., Ltd. (Hangzhou): This company specializes in the R&D and production of fluid transmission equipment. Its products are widely used in petrochemical, military nuclear power, new energy, and environmental sectors. They hold the top market share domestically and are exported to over 50 countries and regions, including Europe, America, and the Middle East. Depam has achieved significant breakthroughs in crucial core technologies in fluid equipment, owning over 80 patents, including 17 invention patents, and pioneering high-pressure tubular progression pumps, breaking foreign monopolies in the industrial chain of oil and gas extraction and transportation.

Hunan Jinxin Electronic Technology Co., Ltd. (Changsha): Founded just ten years ago, this company, staffed predominantly by specialized technical personnel, has broken the foreign technological monopoly on high-end control DSP (Digital Signal Processor) chip design. It has successfully developed a series of 32-bit fixed-point, 32-bit floating-point, and 16-bit fixed-point digital signal processing products, such as AD32, AVP32, and ADP16, leading in domestic DSP chip shipments and market share. It possesses advanced software and hardware design platforms and a specialized, high-quality DSP design team.

Guangzhou Rigal Electronics Co., Ltd. (Guangzhou): Established in 2013, this company focuses on LCD smart projection, becoming a benchmark enterprise in the domestic projector industry after ten years of development. It owns two independent brands, "Rigal" and "Xianqi," breaking through the technical bottlenecks of the projector industry and pioneering active closure technology in the field, leading a new direction in the domestic smart projection industry. Integrating scientific research, production, brand marketing, and application services, its technological reserves and R&D investment are ahead in the industry. With a global marketing service network, its products are sold in over 30 countries and regions, with 2022 revenue exceeding 500 million yuan and tax payments reaching 18 million yuan.

Shenzhen Xinglian Tiantong Technology Co., Ltd. (Shenzhen): Founded in 2017, this company specializes in "integrated communication and navigation" products and solutions for satellite communication and positioning, aiming to fill gaps in China's satellite application field. Its clients are mainly in emergency transportation, fisheries, electric power, and railways. Using Xinglian Tiantong and Beidou's communication and positioning solutions, domestically produced satellite communication chips, in-house developed satellite communication products, and dispatch management platforms, it provides emergency support services for local fishermen, supplying over 38% of maritime communication satellite terminals for the marine fisheries markets in Zhejiang and Fujian provinces in the past two years.

Suzhou Extreme Vision Robotics Technology Co., Ltd. (Suzhou): Established in 2016, it has become a world-leading binocular vision perception control company. Gathering renowned experts from various fields such as vision, control, artificial intelligence, and agricultural plant protection worldwide, it holds 67 invention patents. It has established platforms like the Multicopter UAV Perception Control Platform (EAP), Low-Speed Outdoor Environment Unmanned Vehicle Perception Control Platform (EGP), and High-Precision Image Inspection Platform (EPP). Solving common difficulties in binocular vision applications such as ghosting, glare, focus, and real-time calibration has made its products popular nationwide and in emerging countries like India and Brazil.

5.3.3 Clustered Development of SMEs with Distinctive Industries

Michael Porter introduced the concept of "industry clusters" in "The Competitive Advantage of Nations" (1990), also known as "industry sounds" or "competitive clusters," defined as "a group of interconnected companies, suppliers, associated industries, and specialized institutions in a particular field within a specific region." Porter argued that clusters reduce transaction costs, improve efficiency, and enhance incentives, creating collective wealth such as information, specialized institutions, and reputation. More importantly, clusters improve the conditions for innovation, accelerate productivity growth, and are more conducive to forming new enterprises. In modern economic development, enterprises within industrial clusters primarily engage in product development, production, and sales activities around a unified or closely related industry. Individual enterprises within clusters are primarily small and medium-sized but collectively possess significant scale advantages and high market share.

In recent years, to enhance the competitive capabilities of SMEs, the Chinese government has begun to summarize the typical experiences of clustered SME development and formulate policy measures to nurture SME clusters within distinctive industries, guiding clustered development. In 2022, the Ministry of Industry and Information Technology formulated the "Interim Measures for Promoting the Development of SME Distinctive Industry Clusters," proposing to cultivate SME industry clusters with strong core competitiveness within county-level administrative divisions, centering on SMEs through industry aggregation, highlighting advantages and characteristics, pooling resources, building collaboration networks, and improving governance services. Specific requirements include: (1) precisely selecting dominant industries for clusters, forming complete industrial chains, enhancing specialization and supporting capabilities, promoting collaborative development among large, medium, and small enterprises, strengthening the tiered cultivation of high-quality SMEs, and building advanced manufacturing industry clusters; (2) constructing multi-level industry cluster technology innovation platforms, integrating basic infrastructure and service resources for technology innovation, promoting cooperation mechanisms for technology innovation between SME clusters and large enterprises, higher education institutions, and research institutes, and achieving innovation and breakthroughs in common technologies; (3) accelerating the digital transformation of industry clusters, enhancing the construction of new types of information infrastructure, establishing a comprehensive industrial internet system, promoting intelligent manufacturing equipment, standards, and system solutions, building information resource sharing platforms, and improving the digitalization level of industry clusters; and (4) accelerating the green and low-carbon transformation of industry clusters, adjusting and optimizing the energy consumption structure of industry clusters, promoting the application of new and clean energy, undertaking energy-saving and green low-carbon technological transformations, strengthening the comprehensive utilization of resources and pollution control, and constructing a relatively complete green manufacturing system. Thus, the goal of building SME distinctive industry clusters is not only to construct SME clusters with deepened industrial division and configuration, leveraging production scale advantages, information sharing benefits, and technological spillover effects, but also to accelerate the digital and green low-carbon transformation of SME clusters.

In 2023, the Ministry of Industry and Information Technology organized provinces, cities, and autonomous regions to inspect, recommend, and identify 100 SME distinctive industry clusters as typical representatives nationwide. These clusters are: First, aggregating a group of high-quality SMEs, with nearly 30,000 SMEs settling in these 100 distinctive industry clusters, including 1,487 specialized and sophisticated SMEs, 294 specialized and sophisticated "little giants," and 5,000 innovative SMEs, achieving an industrial total output value of 1.8 trillion yuan. Second, playing a strong and complementary role in the industrial supply chains, each industry cluster has formed integrated and relatively stable industrial and supply chains, especially achieving a high level of specialized supporting capabilities in key segments such as high-performance materials, smart chips, precision devices, new energy vehicle power systems, and industrial robots. Third, driving rapid regional economic development, with the dominant industries of these clusters becoming the pillar industries of local economic development, significantly contributing to local economic growth.

5.3.3.1 SME Distinctive Industry Cluster Examples

Shenzhen Longhua District New Display Devices Industry Cluster: After three years of development, this cluster has gathered over 60 SMEs and holds significant advantages in key components and materials such as polarizers, LCD panels, small-pitch LEDs, modules, and panel manufacturing equipment. It houses "little giant" companies such as Chaptech Optoelectronics, Haidemen Electronics, Baode Computers, H&T, and Guangyue Technology. It initially formed a startup ecosystem led by leading companies and an SME congregation, along with information resource sharing and a division of labor development pattern. In 2022, the cluster achieved a total output value of 31.075 billion yuan, with new display devices accounting for 98.7% of the cluster's total output value.

Shanghai Minhang District Gene Industry Cluster: By mapping out the industry, continuously perfecting the industrial support chain, and strengthening collaboration with neighboring universities, a closed-loop and coupling effect of the industrial ecological cluster has been formed. It has gathered over 250 SMEs, including over 40 chain-leading companies, over 75 specialized and sophisticated enterprises, and more than 30 leading companies in gene industry sub-fields. Based on chain-leading enterprises, an upstream, midstream, and downstream industrial chain relationship in critical gene testing and diagnosis areas has been established. Over the past two years, the leading industry's revenue growth rate has reached 40.26%, with the cluster's total revenue exceeding 22 billion yuan in 2022.

Hunan Shaodong Lighter Industry Cluster: Formed over more than 30 years of development, it has 114 companies, led by Dongyi Electric Co., Ltd., implementing integrated division of labor from product

R&D, raw material procurement, processing production to packaging. It completes the support of 216 kinds of components and 14 processing technologies within a 20 km radius, relies on the Intelligent Manufacturing Technology Institute for technological development, and solves unified testing, customs declaration, cabinet matching, and transportation issues through the Lighter Industry Association. In 2022, it produced over 15 billion lighters, with an annual output value of 12.5 billion yuan, exporting products to over 120 countries and regions, accounting for about 70% of the global lighter market.

Hebei Gaoyang Towel Textile Industry Cluster: Known as the "Textile Hometown," it has formed an integrated industrial chain including "textile, weaving, printing and dyeing, finishing, and sales," with a supporting system from textile raw materials, weaving machines, accessories supply to design R&D, quality testing, and logistics distribution. There are over 1,000 textile enterprises, 158 textile professional villages, and the largest towel wholesale market in China, holding first place in production and sales volume nationwide, with a market share of over 40%. In 2022, the cluster's output value reached 53 billion yuan, accounting for about 75% of the county's total industrial output. Through design R&D and green transformation, it has created an ecological and environmentally friendly development model for the textile industry.

Fujian Nan'an Plumbing and Sanitary Ware Industry Cluster: After over 40 years of development, it has formed an integrated plumbing and sanitary ware industry cluster, including technology R&D, processing production, and assembly packaging. There are over 700 SMEs, covering over 3,000 varieties such as hardware plumbing, sanitary ceramics, shower rooms, and bathroom cabinets, with an industrial output value exceeding 30 billion yuan in 2022. Actively promoting the intelligence, personalization, and customization of products, integrating related enterprises to provide whole-house decoration solutions, it has obtained over 300 technology and design patents in the smart kitchen and bathroom field, forming standard and brand advantages in the industry.

5.3.4 Digital Transformation of SMEs

The main manifestations of the transition from an industrial society to an information society are: (1) information obtains a real economic existence rather than just being abstract ideas; (2) new inventions in communication and computer technology will shorten the time for information flow; (3) new information technologies are first used to solve old industrial tasks and then gradually create new activities, new methods, and new products; and (4) enterprises provide information goods and services, and the information economy proliferates. In 2016, Richard Baldwin, in his book "The Great Convergence: Information Technology and the New Globalization," analyzed the informatization trend in the process of new globalization, believing that with the arrival of the information and communication technology revolution, new organizational forms will magnify the economic impact of information technology and communication technology. Due to the rise of the internet and increased computing power, complex long-distance collaboration and cooperation have become simpler, faster, cheaper, and more secure, profoundly impacting economic globalization. In recent years, advances in information technology have made new progress, with digital technology and artificial intelligence transforming organizational management methods, providing new opportunities for SME development.

Adapting to the global trend of integration between globalization and informatization, as well as the rise of digital technology and artificial intelligence, the Chinese government guides SMEs to inject new vitality into organizational management changes using network technology and digital technology. This effort aims to inject new energy into the development of traditional and modern industries, especially by actively promoting the deep integration of the digital economy and the real economy, encouraging the application of large artificial intelligence models in vertical fields, striving to improve the refinement level of supply chain management, and enhancing the empowerment of digital economy platform companies to supply-chain enterprises. In November 2022, the Ministry of Industry and Information Technology issued the "Guide for SME Digital Transformation," outlining the basic ideas for guiding SMEs to accelerate digital transformation.

(1) SMEs objectively assess their digital state and clarify the direction of digital transformation. This effort involves evaluating the digital base level, enterprise information management level, and internal and external resources for digital transformation. Companies should analyze the potential value and significance of transformation in business and management segments, select digital transformation target levels, and develop plans and implementation schemes to accelerate digital transformation.

(2) Through digital transformation in management segments, SMEs enhance the level of refined enterprise management. Companies should build an organizational structure and management system adapted to digital transformation, strengthen digital technology and knowledge training for managers and employees, deepen internal cross-department cooperation and external collaboration through digitization, form a digital application operating mechanism, and promote refined, convenient, and efficient enterprise management.
(3) Through digital transformation in business segments, SMEs achieve the integration of the digital economy and the real economy. Strategies used include incorporating digital technology in R&D design, manufacturing, warehousing logistics, and marketing, implementing product life-cycle digital management, and using subscription services and lightweight products to reduce operational costs. Effectively utilizing internet platforms, industrial internet platforms, and digital transformation service providers, companies develop value-added services based on digital products.
(4) SMEs build collaborative mechanisms for digital transformation by integrating into digital ecosystems. They should actively respond to core enterprises in the industry chain, supply chain, industry-leading enterprises, and industry clusters, achieve collaborative support with industrial internet platforms, and leverage resources such as orders, technology, tools, talent, and knowledge opened by large enterprises and digital service providers to explore symbiotic and shared cooperation models.

Recently a questionnaire survey was conducted on SME digital transformation, analyzing the constraints, goal selections, development stages, and basic digital transformation paths for Chinese SMEs.

(1) Constraints on SME digital transformation. About 70% of SMEs have a positive attitude towards digital transformation, about 20% are observing, and about 10% have a negative attitude. Digital transformation involves not only technological change but also adjustments to business models. Due to a lack of digital cognition among all enterprise personnel, attitudes towards digitization vary at different levels. Digital transformation requires significant financial investment and demands that employees master corresponding digital technologies, posing a challenge for many companies.

(2) Goal selection for SME digital transformation. Different levels of digital goals are often selected based on the characteristics of different industry business types and current needs. Specifically, traditional labor-intensive SMEs, due to low profit margins and low employee knowledge and technical levels, choose shallow digital goals; marketing-driven SMEs in the food and home industries, although having a great need for online platforms, choose moderate digital goals due to modest profit margins; technology R&D-driven and retail and service SMEs, due to robust demand for digital technology and online platforms, choose deep digital goals.

(3) Development stages of SME digital transformation. Limited by the degree of demand, financial strength, and employee quality, SME digital transformation will go through different development stages, progressively climbing from lower to higher levels. The first level involves basic business process organization and standard data management, using simple information technology applications; the second level uses information technology means or management tools to achieve digital management of a single business; the third level applies information systems and digital technology for data analysis, achieving digital management of all main businesses; the fourth level uses data integration analysis across the entire business chain to achieve data-driven business collaboration and intelligent decision-making.

(4) Basic approaches to SME digital transformation. This transformation involves a systematic engineering of internal management and external collaboration. Its main paths are: firstly, improving the digital technology level of business managers and employees, which is a core requirement of digital transformation; secondly, building basic information network infrastructure and digital tools, which are necessary conditions for digital transformation; thirdly, relying on quality digital service providers and service platforms, which are social services for digital transformation; and fourthly, leveraging government and societal mutual aid infrastructure and environments, which form the ecosystem for digital transformation.

5.3.4.1 SME Digital Transformation Exemplary Cases

Hunan Xiangtan Hengxin Industrial Co., Ltd.: Specializing in underground mining transportation equipment, the company has been advancing digital transformation since 2018, focusing on developing platforms, implementing intelligent manufacturing, and innovating management. Based on IoT, it built an "Industrial Internet Control Platform" offering real-time monitoring, operation forecasting, remote intelligent fault diagnosis, and digital operation services based on cloud computing. Its digital transformation through online platform construction significantly improved specialized manufacturing and service levels, saving management costs and preventing safety accidents and breakdown losses.

Jiangsu Deyuan Pharmaceutical Co., Ltd.: Mainly producing oral solid dosage forms, the company has implemented digital, networked, and intelligent transformations in recent years. On top of mature ERP and Warehouse Management Systems (WMS), it manages the entire production process with an online Manufacturing Execution System (MES), standardizing the whole production flow through informatized management, realizing standardized manufacturing processes, integrated workshop management, digital equipment operation, and refined quality control, and building a visual information display platform, thereby enhancing production efficiency and product quality stability.

Henan Zhonghuang Energy Saving Electrical Appliances Co., Ltd.: Specializing in electric heating equipment, the company started building a digital platform integrating R&D, production, sales, and service in 2016. By constructing carbon fiber heating systems, Zhonghuang cloud control systems, and ERP systems, it formed a complete life-cycle informatization management process from demand, planning, design, production, distribution, operation, use, maintenance, and recycling. Through interconnecting data across procurement, warehouse, finance, production, and business segments, it promoted internal data communication, resource sharing, and business collaboration within the industry chain, improving production efficiency and service quality.

Inner Mongolia Duowell Biotech Co., Ltd.: Since 2016, the company has mainly produced perlite products. It has undergone three rounds of automation upgrades in its production process, achieving an automatic data collection rate and automatic control usage rate of 80% for crucial production steps. These upgrades significantly reduced the product's comprehensive cost and increased productivity.

Heilongjiang Jiu San Agricultural Reclamation Beidahuang Potato Industry Co., Ltd.: Mainly engaged in the food processing industry, it began a digital transformation in 2021, establishing a highly automated, digital, visualized, procedural, and model-based potato food production workshop. This workshop allows real-time monitoring of the milling process and dynamic optimization based on production information. Adopting an intelligent optimization control system for starch production reduced energy costs by about 15% per ton and environmental protection costs by over 50%, achieving considerable economic and social benefits.

5.4 Conclusion

Global trends significantly impact countries of all sizes, with profound implications for super-large countries. These trends include prompting governments to implement domestic and international openness, providing entrepreneurs with superior business environments, encouraging SMEs to adapt to globalization and informatization trends, and achieving enterprise and industry transformation and upgrading.

Since entering the 21st century and joining the World Trade Organization, China has embarked on a comprehensive opening-up process, moving from partial to comprehensive external openness and from trade, investment, and financial sectors to institutional openness. This external openness, in turn, drives domestic openness, demanding regions to break down blockades and barriers, forming an integrated domestic market, allowing SMEs to compete fairly and enter and exit freely in this vast market, thereby stimulating entrepreneurial and innovative vitality. After 20-plus years of reform and exploration, China's openness and business environment ranking have continuously climbed, now approaching the levels of developed countries like Japan and leading among developing countries.

SMEs are the mainstay of entrepreneurship and a vital force in China's economic development. To promote the development of SMEs, the Chinese government has enacted laws and regulations to protect and support SMEs and formulated policies and measures to strengthen them. In recent years, Chinese SMEs have adapted to globalization and informatization trends, strengthening technological innovation, industrial upgrading, and management transformation. Three significant characteristics have emerged: Firstly, improving the overall quality of SMEs, advancing specialization, precision management, and technological innovation, cultivating a batch of modern SMEs with specialization, refinement, uniqueness, and innovation, and guiding the trend of national economic development. Secondly, accelerating the clustered development of SMEs, guiding SMEs to form regional distinctive industry clusters according to the law of industry agglomeration and scale efficiency, cultivating a batch of SME industry clusters with complete industrial and supply chains around leading industries, and guiding the trend of industry agglomeration development. Thirdly, accelerating the digital transformation of SMEs, adapting to the characteristics of information technology, digital technology, and artificial intelligence development, advancing network platform construction and enterprise management mode transformation, cultivating a batch of modern SMEs that integrate digital technology into the entire process of R&D design, production manufacturing, and logistics marketing, guiding the trend of a digital economy empowering the real economy.

References

Baldwin, R. (2016). *The Great Convergence: Information Technology and the New Globalization*. Cambridge: Harvard University Press.

China Academy of High-Tech Industry Economic Research. (2023) *Analysis of 100 SME Distinctive Industry Clusters in 2022*. Available at: https://ythxxfb.miit.gov.cn/ythzxfwpt/hlwmh/tzgg/sbfw/qyshzr/art/2023/art_5295068028f54138a9ced3a8347da4ee.html [accessed May 21, 2024].

China Industrial Newspaper. (2022). *Typical Cases of SME Digital Transformation in 2021 Unveiled*. Available at: www.cics-cert.org.cn/web_root/webpage/articlecontent_101003_1514845390388596738.html [accessed May 21, 2024].

Economic Daily. (2024). *Supporting SMEs to Focus on Specialization, Finesse, Uniqueness, and Innovation*. Available at: www.miit.gov.cn/threestrategy/dtzx/tpz/art/2024/art_9c910333de044fc7961fd4df8e692d52.html [accessed May 21, 2024].

Greeven, M. (2021). *Chinese Innovation: Business Models of New Innovative Enterprises*. Beijing: CITIC Publishing.

He Min, and Zhen Feng. (2021). *Digital Interpretation of China*. China Renmin University Press.

Ministry of Finance, Ministry of Industry and Information Technology. (2021) *Notice on Supporting the High-Quality Development of 'Specialized, Fine, Unique, and Innovative' SMEs*. Available at: www.gov.cn/zhengce/zhengceku/2021-02/03/content_5584629.htm [accessed May 21, 2024].

Ministry of Industry and Information Technology. (2022). *2022 Annual Report on the Development Environment Assessment of SMEs*. Available at: www.miit.gov.cn/xwdt/gxdt/sjdt/art/2023/art_e0b3a6eb45e343c492c80907de731283.html [accessed May 21, 2024].

Ministry of Industry and Information Technology. (2022). *Guidelines for the Digital Transformation of SMEs*. Available at: chrome-extension://bnjoienjhhclcabnkbhhfndecoipmcdg/background/jgpdf/layout/index.html?file=https://www.gov.cn/zhengce/zhengceku/2022-11/09/5725642/files/71a18505f65e401fa242dca9e263839c.pdf [accessed May 21, 2024].

Ministry of Industry and Information Technology. (2022). *Interim Measures for Promoting the Development of SME Distinctive Industry Clusters*. Available at: www.gov.cn/zhengce/zhengceku/2022-09/14/content_5709725.htm [accessed May 21, 2024].

Ministry of Industry and Information Technology. (2022) *SME Digital Level Assessment Indicators*. Available at: www.gov.cn/zhengce/zhengceku/2022-11/12/content_5726411.htm [accessed May 21, 2024].

National Information Security Development Research Center & CICS-CERT National Industrial Information Security Center. (2021). *Typical Cases of Digital Transformation of Chinese SMEs*. Available at: https://cics-cert.org.cn/web_root/webpage/page_content_104005.html [accessed May 21, 2024].

Ouyang, Y. (2009). *Research on the Policy and Service System for the Development of SMEs in China*. Beijing: China Social Sciences Press.

Ouyang, Y., Yi, X., and Tang, L. (2019). *Growth and Transformation of Emerging Powers: Research on BRICS Economies*. London: Palgrave Macmillan Press.

Ouyang, Y. (2022). *Large Countries' Development Path: Experience and Theory*. Berlin: Springer Press.

People's Posts and Telecommunications News. (2022) *MIIT Fully Advances SME Digital Transformation*. Available at: https://paper.cnii.com.cn/article/rmydb_16221_312398.html [accessed May 21, 2024].

Porter, M. (1990). *The Competitive Advantage of Nations*. New York: The Free Press.

Schumacher, F. (1973). *Small Is Beautiful*. Blon and Briggs Press.

State Administration for Market Regulation. (2023). *Anti-Monopoly Law of the People's Republic of China*. Available at: www.samr.gov.cn/zw/zfxxgk/fdzdgknr/fgs/art/2023/art_f0fae9eb3a684fc39e84d89eabfc2caa.html [accessed May 21, 2024].

State Council of the People's Republic of China. (2022). *Opinions of the CPC Central Committee and the State Council on Accelerating the Construction of a Unified National Market*. Available at: www.gov.cn/gongbao/content/2022/content_5687499.htm [accessed May 21, 2024].

State Council of the People's Republic of China. (2021). *Cultivating 'Specialized, Fine, Unique, and Innovative' SMEs Achieves Positive Results*. Available at: www.gov.cn/xinwen/2021-11/23/content_5652843.htm [accessed May 21, 2024].

State Council of the People's Republic of China. (2019). *Regulations on Optimizing the Business Environment.* Available at: www.gov.cn/zhengce/content/2019-10/23/content_5443963.htm [accessed May 21, 2024].

Tang, L., Ouyang, Y., and Hong, L. (2022). *Economic Opening Strategy of Emerging Major Countries: China's Scheme for Building an Open World Economy*. Peking: Peking University Press.

The Department of Industrial Policy and Regulations of the Ministry of Industry and Information Technology of the People's Republic of China. (2017). *SME Promotion Law of the People's Republic of China (2017 Revision)*. Available at: https://wap.miit.gov.cn/zwgk/zcwj/flfg/art/2022/art_ab42845190ca49c797f8d8d31e700fc9.html [accessed May 21, 2024].

The General Office of the State Council of the People's Republic of China. (2022) *State Council General Office on Further Optimizing the Business Environment and Reducing Systemic Transaction Costs for Market Entities*. Available at: www.gov.cn/zhengce/content/2022-09/15/content_5709962.htm [accessed May 21, 2024].

World Bank. (2020). Doing Business 2020 Report. Available at: https://documents1.worldbank.org/curated/en/688761571934946384/pdf/Doing-Business-2020-Comparing-Business-Regulation-in-190-Economies.pdf [accessed May 21, 2024].

Vaisbitt, J. (1982). *Megatrends: The New Directions Transforming Our Lives*. New York: Warner Books

6 China's Major Companies and Entrepreneurial Spirit

Yao Ouyang

6.1 Chinese Companies in the Fortune Global 500

The growth of the large companies has fostered an entrepreneurial spirit in China, leading to the emergence of modern entrepreneurs who are market-driven, committed to innovation and excellence, and dedicated to fulfilling social responsibilities. This entrepreneurial spirit is a precious resource for entrepreneurship, innovation, and socio-economic development.

Leveraging its status as a late-developing major country, including advantages in factor endowments, technology catch-up, and market size, China has promoted enterprise innovation and entrepreneurship, nurturing a series of advanced giant enterprises. China is home to 142 companies in Fortune Magazine's 2023 Fortune Global 500 list, with these entities achieving total operating revenue of 11.78 billion USD. Finance, transportation, telecommunications, and high-tech enterprises have achieved a sales return rate of over 5%, making them exemplary representatives of world-class businesses and China's advanced large-scale companies. We have conducted a comprehensive analysis of these companies, focusing on their affiliations, industry distribution, operating revenue, and average profits, to understand the basic situation of China's giant companies.

(1) The Affiliation of Chinese Companies: Diversification Trend. The affiliations of the Chinese companies show a trend towards diversification, with state-owned enterprises (SOEs) accounting for 69.31% of the total and private enterprises making up only 31.69%. The majority are SOEs affiliated with different governments and departments, with 40.84% affiliated with the national government and

DOI: 10.4324/9781003602378-10

27.46% with local governments. The number of private enterprises is relatively small, as most are small and medium-sized enterprises (SMEs), and their growth and expansion require a long-term process.

(2) Industry Distribution of Chinese Companies: Diversification Trend. The industry distribution of Chinese companies listed can be categorized into three tiers, from highest to lowest. The first tier includes the finance, metals, and energy sectors, mainly controlled by the state and government; the second tier includes industrial manufacturing, engineering and construction, technology services, commercial services, automotive, and logistics and transportation sectors, where state-owned and private enterprises develop side by side; the third tier includes logistics and transportation, real estate, aerospace, chemicals, public utilities, as well as food and healthcare industries, mainly related to people's livelihoods. Compared to 2000, the financial, energy, and technology sectors have proliferate=d (Figure 6.1).

(3) Operating Revenue of Chinese Companies: Upward Trend. The total operating revenue of Chinese companies entering the Fortune Global 500 has grown rapidly, indicating ongoing expansion in production and sales scale. The first phase, from 2009 to 2014, saw total operating revenue increase from about 2 trillion USD to about 6 trillion USD; the second phase, from 2014 to 2023, saw it rise from about 6 trillion USD to about 12 trillion USD (Figure 6.2). Clearly, both stages maintained a momentum of rapid and sustained growth.

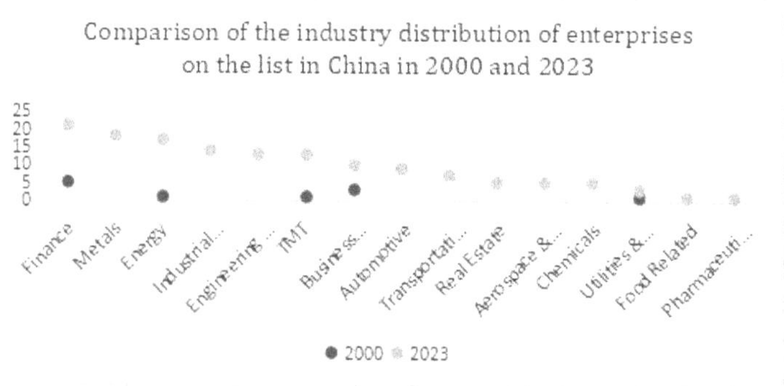

Figure 6.1 Comparison of industry distribution of Chinese companies listed in 2000 and 2023.

Source: Author according to Fortune 500 Analysis 2023 published by CU.

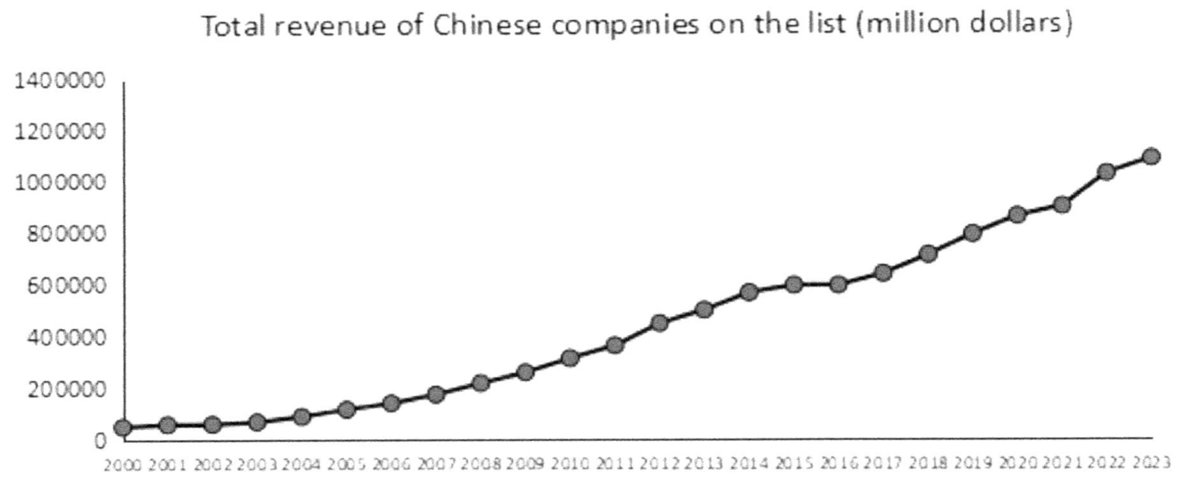

Figure 6.2 Change in total operating revenue of Chinese companies listed (in ten thousands USD).

Source: Author according to Fortune 500 Analysis 2023 published by CU.

Figure 6.3 Average revenue and profit by industry of Chinese companies listed in 2023 (in million USD).

Source: Based on Fortune 500 Analysis 2023 published by CU Consulting. URL: www.mpgroup.cn.

(4) Average Profit of Chinese Companies: Non-uniform Trend. The Chinese companies are distributed across many industries, with significant differences in average profits (Figure 6.3). The first tier is the financial sector, with exceptionally high average profits; the second tier includes the technology, media, and communications sector, with relatively high average profits; the third tier includes transportation and logistics, with lower average profits. Overall, this presents a non-uniform structure and trend.

6.2 Comprehensive Analysis of China's Top 500 Enterprises

The "China Top 500 Enterprises Development Report," published by the China Enterprise Confederation, represents China's leading enterprises. Chinese scholar Xinjian Cui conducted a detailed evaluation based on five dimensions: scale economy, economic efficiency, technology innovation, brand value, and internationalization level. According to the data provided in the report, the development status of these enterprises reflects the development level, main characteristics, and fundamental trends of China's leading enterprises.

(1) The overall scale of enterprises has grown significantly. From 2010 to 2019, the total assets increased from 91.28 trillion yuan to 299.15 trillion yuan, expanding about threefold; total operating revenue grew from 27.64 trillion yuan to 79.10 trillion yuan, nearly tripling; and the number of employees increased from 27.0195 million to 33.5911 million, expanding by about a quarter
(2) The economic efficiency of enterprises has slightly declined. Between 2010 and 2019, the per capita operating revenue of large Chinese enterprises showed an upward trend, increasing from about 1 million yuan to about 2.5 million yuan, a 2.5-fold increase; the net asset profit rate remained essentially unchanged, but the income profit rate decreased from about 5.5% to about 4.5%. These data indicate that large Chinese enterprises still mainly rely on low-price advantages for market competition without improving economic efficiency.
(3) Continuous increase in R&D investment by enterprises. From 2010 to 2019, R&D investment by China's top 500 enterprises continuously increased from about 350 billion yuan to about 900 billion yuan, approximately a 2.5-fold increase; however, in terms of research intensity, i.e., the ratio of R&D investment to the total value of production, the increase was relatively small, only from about 1.5% to about 1.65%. These results indicate that although R&D investment continues to increase with the expansion of enterprise production scale, the growth of research intensity could be faster, indicating a problem of insufficient investment in R&D.
(4) Gradual increase in enterprise brand value. Between 2010 and 2019, the structure of the proportion of brands within various brand value ranges underwent new changes. Specifically, brands with a value of less than 10 billion yuan gradually decreased, while the number of brands within all ranges above 10 billion yuan continuously increased. The number of brands valued between 10 billion and 20 billion yuan showed a trend of first increasing and then decreasing. In comparison, the number of brands valued above 20 billion yuan exhibited a continuous upward trend. These observations demonstrate a positive correlation between brand value and the increase in enterprise scale.
(5) Steady progress in the internationalization of enterprises. From 2011 to 2019, the proportion of overseas employees in Chinese multinational companies continued to increase, the proportion of overseas assets showed a steady trend, the proportion of overseas

operating income slightly declined in recent years, and the transnational index of enterprises slightly increased. This indicates that the international operations of Chinese enterprises are steadily developing, but as the domestic market scale expands, large Chinese enterprises rely more on the large domestic market. The proportion or degree of internationalization of these enterprises' overseas operations is not particularly high.

In summary, Chinese enterprises have gradually grown more vital in exploring domestic and international markets and accumulating technology, brand value, and profits. However, overall, compared to world-class enterprises, Chinese top enterprises still have some gaps:

(1) The industrial structure of Chinese enterprises needs optimization. The main businesses of Chinese enterprises with high operating income are concentrated in engineering and construction, mining and crude oil, financial insurance trade, and real estate. In contrast, American enterprises' main businesses with high operating income are focused on computers, aviation, semiconductors, commerce, insurance, and food. Compared, China still has a significant gap in high-tech fields and needs to accelerate the development of industries such as information technology, computer software, internet services, semiconductors, electronic components, and commercial insurance, especially by focusing on improving the specialization level in these fields.

(2) The economic efficiency of Chinese enterprises needs improvement. Comparing the economic efficiency of enterprises in major countries of the Fortune Global 500 in 2019, Chinese enterprises' economic efficiency is on the same level as that of Japan and France and slightly lower than that of the UK and Germany. For example, the net asset profit rate is 9.93%, lower than the United States 15.12%, the UK's 10.37%, and Germany's 10.19%, on par with Japan's 9.90%, and higher than France's 8.18%; the income profit rate is 5.20%, lower than the United States' 7.77%, the UK's 7.75%, on par with Japan's 5.19%, and higher than France's 4.81% and Germany's 4.35%; the per capita operating income is 379,500 USD/person, lower than the US's 548,000 USD/person, the UK's 446,700 USD/person, and on par with Germany's 387,100 USD/person

and France's 378,400 USD/person. However, compared to the United States, there is still a significant gap, with a 5.19% lower net asset profit rate, a 2.57% lower income profit rate, and a 179,100 USD/person lower per capita operating income.

(3) The R&D intensity of Chinese enterprises needs to be increased. In recent years, the Chinese government and enterprises have increased R&D investment to promote the technological level of industries. From 2019 to 2023, R&D expenditure increased from 2,214.4 billion yuan to 3,327.8 billion yuan, with an average annual growth of more than 10%. By the end of 2023, there were 4.99 million valid invention patents, an increase of 18.5% over the previous year. Between 2010 and 2019, the total R&D investment in the United States increased from 367.5 billion USD to 612.7 billion USD, maintaining the global lead; China's R&D investment rose from 39.8 billion USD to 514.8 billion USD, moving up to second place globally. However, the R&D intensity of China's top 500 enterprises is only about 1.6%, while companies like Huawei reach 10%, Uten Table Co. 15.7%, Amazon 12.4%, and Samsung Electronics 7.5%. Clearly, large Chinese enterprises still need to increase their efforts and intensity in technological R&D.

(4) The brand value of Chinese enterprises needs to be enhanced. According to data from the World Brand Lab's "2018 World's 500 Most Valuable Brands" report, China had 37 brands listed, fewer than the United States with 223, the UK with 42, France with 43, and Japan with 39. In terms of the average age of the brands, Chinese brands averaged 53 years, significantly younger than those from the UK at 163 years, France at 118 years, Germany at 105 years, Japan at 94 years, and the United States at 92 years. Regarding the industry structure of brand enterprises, the UK, Germany, and Japan are mainly concentrated in the automotive and parts industry, the United States is in the media industry, and China is mainly in the energy sector. In summary, the quantity and structure of Chinese brands still need to be strengthened and optimized.

(5) The degree of internationalization of Chinese enterprises needs further expansion. According to data from the United Nations Conference on Trade and Development's "World Investment Report 2019," among the world's top 500 multinational companies, the transnational index of Chinese enterprises was 21.45,

significantly lower than the United States at 45.06, the UK at 81.64, France at 63.90, Germany at 63.04, Japan at 56.10, and again the United States at 45.06. The "2022 China Multinational Companies Top 100 Transnational Index" report released by the China Enterprise Confederation shows that the average transnational index of these 100 Chinese multinational companies is 15.59%, with overseas assets accounting for 17.06%, overseas operating income for 19.65%, and overseas employees for 10.05%. Although showing an upward trend, the degree of internationalization still needs to be strengthened compared to enterprises from developed countries.

6.3 Technological Innovation and Entrepreneurial Path of Large Enterprises

A list of pioneering Chinese enterprises is presented: from the first wave of entrepreneurship between 1984 and 1989 emerged giant enterprises such as Haier, Huawei, Lenovo, and Sany Group; from the second wave of entrepreneurship between 1999 and 2010 emerged giants like Alibaba, Baidu, Tencent, and Xiaom (Table 6.1).

These giant enterprises are internationally recognized as pioneering and quality companies, and their entrepreneurial processes represent the entrepreneurial journey of China's large enterprises. Analyzing the development paths of these successful enterprises reveals that they follow a similar entrepreneurial logic: they rely on China's vast domestic market to expand their scale and cultivate innovation capabilities and on advanced core technologies to nurture businesses and explore markets. They grow based on the market size advantages of an emerging major country, relying on the local market before embarking on internationalization, bolstered by enhanced technological innovation capabilities. Specifically, Chinese enterprises can be roughly divided into two types: the first type, represented by Huawei, is a "technology + market" type, taking a path driven by technology; the second type, represented by Xiaomi, is a "market + technology" type, taking a path where the market drives technology.

(1) Huawei's Innovation and Entrepreneurial Path

Huawei Technologies Co., Ltd. is a global leader in information and communications (ICT) infrastructure and smart devices, offering

Table 6.1 China's Pioneering Enterprises: Eastern Giants

2023 Fortune Global 500			
Rank	*Country*	*Number of Top-Ranked Companies*	*Continent*
1	China	142	Asia
2	United States	136	Americas
3	Japan	41	Asia
4	Germany	30	Europe
5	France	24	Europe
6	South Korea	18	Asia
7	United Kingdom	15	Europe
8	Canada	14	Americas
9	Switzerland	11	Europe
10	Netherlands	10	Europe
11	India	9	Asia
12	Brazil	9	Americas
13	Spain	8	Europe
14	Italy	5	Europe
15	Russia	3	Europe
16	Singapore	3	Asia
17	Ireland	3	Europe
18	Denmark	3	Europe
19	Mexico	3	Americas
20	Australia	2	Oceania
21	Sweden	1	Europe
22	Indonesia	1	Asia
23	Norway	1	Europe
24	Saudi Arabia	1	Asia
25	Malaysia	1	Asia
26	Thailand	1	Asia
27	Turkey	1	Asia
28	Austria	1	Europe
29	Belgium	1	Europe
30	Poland	1	Europe
31	Luxembourg	1	Europe

Source: Mark J. Greeven, Chinese Innovation: Business Models for New Innovative Enterprises, CITIC Group Publishing, 2021.

competitive ICT solutions, products, and services with end-to-end solutions in telecommunications operators, enterprise terminals, and cloud computing. Huawei's founder, Ren Zhengfei, focused on technological innovation in the company's early days, developing programmable switching technology for small units and digital exchange technology solutions for rural areas. Entering the 21st century, he established a global technology R&D system, becoming a significant promoter and global leader in 5G technology. At each stage of the company's growth, he has developed new products through technological innovation, thereby exploring product markets. Thus, the "Huawei model" is described as a "technology-driven market" model centered on technology development, exploring product markets through technological innovation.

(2) Huawei's Growth Journey

Founded in Shenzhen in 1987, the firm initially acted as a sales agent for PBXs from a Hong Kong company before independently developing programmable switches for small units. The company then explored rural digital exchange technology solutions, launching the C&C08 digital programmable switch. In 1995, sales reached 1.5 billion yuan; in 1998, sales revenue reached 8.9 billion yuan.

In 1999, Huawei began establishing technology development centers in India, Russia, Sweden, and the United States to collaborate on enterprise data network solutions and develop 4G technology, working with customers in over 30 countries in cloud computing and becoming a major promoter of the EU 5G project. In 2010, sales revenue reached 185.2 billion yuan, entering the Fortune Global 500; in 2015, sales revenue reached 395 billion yuan; in 2020, sales revenue reached 891.5 billion yuan.

In 2019, Huawei was placed on the US Department of Commerce's blacklist, leading Western countries under US influence to stop supplying key components and technology, severely impacting its smartphone business and 5G infrastructure business. Huawei began using its Kirin chips and operating system, achieving significant breakthroughs in imaging, external sound, systems, screens, communication, and chips through independent R&D, thus preventing a significant reduction in market share.

Huawei's growth journey overall shows a characteristic of market development driven by technological innovation. It has obtained many invention patents through integrated innovation and independent R&D, continuously developing new products and exploring vast domestic and overseas markets, embodying the Huawei model and experience.

Huawei has achieved globally recognized success in technology R&D, securing numerous technology patents. Huawei continuously increases its R&D efforts, with R&D expenditure rising from 17.6 billion yuan in 2010 to 161.5 billion yuan in 2022, maintaining about 10% of company revenue over the long term, exceeding 20% in recent years, among the highest levels in China's large enterprises and also ranking high among the Fortune Global 500. According to the World Intellectual Property Organization (WIPO), Huawei filed 6,952 patents in 2021, ranking first among Chinese enterprises. By 2023, Huawei held 120,000 authorized patents globally, over 90% of which were invention patents, including 9,000 standard-essential patents in the 5G field, far exceeding competitors. Through continuous technology R&D, Huawei has maintained a leading position in 3G, 4G, and 5G, becoming a global industry chain leader with its continuous technological innovation advantage.

Huawei implements open innovation, gathering global innovation resources to accelerate technology catching up and surpassing. Huawei's R&D approach is not closed but globally open. Huawei has established over 20 joint innovation centers with leading global operators and formed partnerships with Motorola, IBM, and 11 other companies in future chip design, providing professional technology solutions to customers. Adopting an imitative innovation approach, Huawei quickly learned and followed leading enterprises' technical standards and product features, engaging in independent R&D based on accumulated knowledge, technology, and resources. The company specializes in utilizing global innovation elements and resources during the R&D process, currently employing over 700 mathematicians, more than 800 physicists, and over 120 chemists, along with 6,000 basic research experts and 60,000 engineers from China and around the world, including developed and emerging countries.

Huawei has leveraged its domestic market to expand globally, gradually amassing a vast market share. Initially, Huawei dominated the rural market in China, earning its first pot of gold; then, it moved into urban markets, distributing its products across major Chinese cities. As its sales revenue approached 10 billion yuan, Huawei began to venture into international markets, moving from emerging markets to developed countries. In 2005, Huawei's overseas sales revenue accounted for 58% of its total sales. However, starting in 2019, due to containment efforts by the United States, Huawei's overseas sales revenue slightly declined, dropping to around 37% in 2022, forming a pattern dominated by the domestic market. Moreover, Huawei's market expansion adopted a technology-leading strategy, producing technologically advanced products through imitative innovation, integrated innovation, and independent R&D, gradually expanding into domestic and international markets.

(3) Xiaomi's Innovation and Entrepreneurial Path

Xiaomi Corporation is an innovative technology company focused on high-end smartphones, Internet TVs, and smart home ecosystem construction. Xiaomi's founder, Lei Jun, positioned the company's philosophy as "making life better with technology," focusing on the market and consumer desires to offer consumers a series of high-cost-performance smart manufacturing products. Xiaomi has created smart products like smartphones, air purifiers, portable chargers, and robot vacuum cleaners using modern advanced technology at different times, quickly capturing the market with their popularity among consumers. We call the "Xiaomi model" a "market-driven technology" model centered on market development, exploring technological integration based on understanding the customer market, epitomizing the Xiaomi model and experience.

(4) Xiaomi's Growth Journey

Founded in Beijing in 2010 by a management team of experienced entrepreneurs, the firm initially focused on developing smartphones based on the Android system. It gradually expanded to smart TVs and smart home devices. They attracted fans and users through online sales and word-of-mouth, with sales revenue surpassing 10 billion yuan in 2012 and reaching 63.6 billion yuan in 2014, achieving rapid growth.

In 2014, Xiaomi entered international markets, first achieving success in India, then moving into other Asian countries, European countries, and Latin American markets. Throughout its development, Xiaomi continuously launched new technologies and products through technological R&D, and by investing and collaborating, it established a series of ecosystem companies that offered services in smart hardware, the Internet, and the Internet of Things. In 2017, sales revenue broke through 100 billion yuan.

Successfully listed on the Hong Kong Stock Exchange in 2018, Xiaomi created the largest-scale tech stock IPO in Hong Kong's history. In 2019, it re-entered the high-end smartphone market. It announced its entry into the smart car sector in 2021, clarifying its core around smartphones to build AIOT devices and services, including ecosystem products for a smart life. In 2019, sales revenue reached 200 billion yuan, making it into the Fortune Global 500.

Xiaomi's growth has been miraculous, making it the youngest Fortune Global 500 company in a decade. Its growth process exhibits characteristics of technology innovation driven by market development, utilizing Internet marketing thinking, the explosive product model, and the ecosystem model to capture a broad consumer base and product market.

Xiaomi successfully applied Internet marketing thinking, achieving a commercial social efficiency revolution. They used an Internet development model to build an operating system that is updated weekly, with new features voted on by MIUI community users, greatly mobilizing user participation and a sense of honor, and encouraging word-of-mouth promotion by users. Starting from the initial 100 anonymous users, it gradually developed into a fan base of 100,000 and a primary user group of 300,000, effectively giving Xiaomi a 100,000-strong product development team and a 300,000-strong marketing team. This team has created many unprecedented and stunning products, some considered the optimal solution or even becoming industry standards. Through this team, Xiaomi has gained an enviable good reputation. They established a global Mi fan community, creating a massive global movement from actions like making language packs, thereby continuously increasing Xiaomi's user base and product influence.

Xiaomi successfully established the "explosive product model," achieving continuous innovation in its product series. "Explosive products," as defined by Lei Jun, are "products distinctly different in definition, performance, quality, or price from existing products, greatly exceeding user expectations, and triggering enthusiastic word-of-mouth spread and sales phenomenon-level products." How to create explosive products? They summarized four principles: first, accurately identify user needs; second, exceed expectations with products; third, offer surprising pricing; and fourth, win with efficiency. These explosive products should directly meet unmet user demands, including unexpected performance and price; simultaneously, explosive products have a magical lever effect, efficiently mobilizing the supply chain, team capabilities, market, and user resources, thus quickly generating momentum and driving rapid company growth.

Xiaomi successfully leveraged the "ecosystem model" to comprehensively affect the industrial ecosystem. Xiaomi identified and supported startups that share Xiaomi's values through non-controlling investments, quickly incubating and assisting talented entrepreneurial teams. These teams received all-around support in product definition, design R&D, supply chain resources, and marketing and sales; through a series of outstanding explosive products, these enterprises and industries were transformed, forming a relatively complete ecosystem with Xiaomi's product lines. Starting in 2018, Xiaomi aimed to replicate Xiaomi's ecosystem model across 100 industries in Chinese manufacturing, gradually changing the face of these industries. Currently, there are over 100 hardware product companies that have created hundreds of industry-recognized and consumer-chased explosive products through Xiaomi's vast production line of the world's most extensive consumer-grade Internet of Things, and promoting the emergence of explosive products such as portable chargers, smart bands, air purifiers, robot vacuum cleaners, as well as the successful public listings of companies like Yunmi Technology, Huami Technology, Stone Technology, and Ninebot.

(5) Outstanding explosive products cultivated by Xiaomi's ecosystem

Xiaomi Portable Charger: Mobile power banks related to smartphones were in high demand, yet the market lacked sophisticated and affordable products. Xiaomi decided to tackle this issue through its ecosystem, giving rise to Zimi Technology, which specializes in power banks with the goal of using higher standards while reducing costs. For this purpose, they utilized the world's highest-quality battery cells, added two protective chips, chose a metal casing, and designed the ends with natural curvature to find the optimal design and cost solution. After its launch, this sleek product with a unibody aluminum alloy shell, anodic sandblasting process, and minimalist design was priced at only 69 yuan, selling 600,000 units in the first month, 1.5 million in the second month, and 3 million in the third month, reaching over 10 million units shipped in the first year, becoming Xiaomi's first ecosystem product to hit the ten-million sales mark.

Xiaomi Air Purifier: Targeting the main issues with air purifiers on the market, such as misleading features, poor functionality despite numerous features, and unattractive design, Xiaomi persuaded Zhimi Technology to focus first on purifying functionality. They used a three-layer filter that could absorb over 90% of PM2.5 particles; they changed from a flat to a tower structure with cylindrical filters to widen the ventilation area, equipped with dual fans on the top and bottom, creating strong airflow to suck in air; this structure allowed air to diffuse in all directions at 270 degrees, flowing through the ceiling, walls, and floor before being sucked back into the purifier, achieving overall room air purification. Its attractive design, compact size, and sufficient power, priced at only 899 yuan per unit, achieved the number one ranking in the consumer interaction index, online reputation index, brand awareness, and market share.

Mi Home Robot Vacuum: Stone Technology, a Xiaomi ecosystem company, carefully observed the market and found that the household penetration rate of robot vacuums was low, transitioning from "random collision" to "path planning" types. Seizing the opportunity of an unsettled market landscape and unoccupied consumer minds, they considered designing and producing top-tier robot vacuum products, defining the product to use mature technology to enhance reliability. They eliminated the mopping and air purification functions found in other robots on the market, focusing solely on cleaning thoroughly and quickly. The LDS (Laser Distance Sensor) was prominently placed in the "eye" on top of the product and paired with image sensors from an American company, giving it a faster cleaning speed. Their meticulously designed products exceeded expectations. In 2016, the Mi Home Robot Vacuum was launched for 1699 yuan, quickly winning consumer favor and rapidly capturing the domestic market.

6.4 Chinese Entrepreneurs and Entrepreneurial Spirit

(1) Innovation Activities and Entrepreneurial Spirit

Joseph Schumpeter, the pioneer of innovation economics, proposed that "economic development stems from innovation," suggesting that economic development requires recombining existing various elements into new combinations. We refer to the realization of new combinations as "enterprises" and people whose function is to realize these new combinations as "entrepreneurs." Innovation in economic development takes five forms, including adopting a new product and production method, opening a new market, offering a new source of raw materials, and achieving a new industrial organization. However, entrepreneurs face three challenges when engaging in innovation activities: first, entrepreneurial innovation exploration disrupts old entities, making existing data information lose its value; second, humans are conservative in many cases, and society usually shows resistance to practices or behaviors contrary to traditional habits; and third, new attempts are inevitably constrained by the social environment, especially facing greater resistance in undeveloped ideological regions. Therefore, entrepreneurs must have the strength and courage to challenge conventional ways of doing things, disregarding traditional forces, a feat few achieve. Thus, entrepreneurs driving economic development emerge from the existing social system as "ideal types" with a unique temperament, driven by three non-hedonistic motives: the first is having dreams and ideals, desiring to find a tempting private kingdom that can garner social prestige; the second is having impulse and will, wishing to prove superiority over others through success and victory; the third is enjoying the pleasure of creation, reveling in the joy of exercising personal abilities and demonstrating talent.

According to Schumpeter, entrepreneurship is a function, and individuals are only true entrepreneurs when they realize new combinations. Therefore, the entrepreneurial spirit embodies the mental qualities required for engaging in entrepreneurial and innovative activities. Following Schumpeter's work, most economists and non-economists have accepted his view of entrepreneurship as "innovation"; it is a unique, innovative element and the driving force behind business innovation and development. Surrounding entrepreneurship and innovation, many scholars interpret the entrepreneurial spirit from different perspectives, such as the spirit of adventure, creativity, dedication, and contractual spirit, as well as qualities of boldness, strength, initiative, energy, foresight, insight, curiosity, perseverance, execution, and organizational coordination. According to the principal component analysis method, entrepreneurship can be summarized as the spirit of dedication, contractual spirit, innovative spirit, entrepreneurial spirit, adventurous spirit, dedication, and openness.

(2) Traditional Culture and Entrepreneurial Spirit

Throughout Chinese history, many outstanding merchants and entrepreneurs adhered to traditional Chinese culture, embodying what is known as the "Confucian merchant spirit." Exceptional Chinese entrepreneurs have always emphasized moral integrity and talent, requiring not only the traits necessary for business and enterprise management, such as shrewdness and the ability to seize opportunities, but also adherence to traditional moral standards, such as perseverance, balancing righteousness and profit, honesty and trustworthiness, and harmonious interpersonal relations. Specifically, they embody the following contents and spirits:

The spirit of unyielding self-improvement. The ancient Chinese text "I Ching" states: "As heaven maintains vigor through movements, a gentleman should constantly strive for self-improvement." This means that just as the heavens move with strength and vigor, gentlemen should, correspondingly, pursue progress and be steadfast and unyielding, always moving forward to achieve unity with the heavens. Entrepreneurs, or Confucians, should first possess the spirit of unyielding self-improvement, have the enterprising spirit of innovation and entrepreneurship, actively plan and advance their endeavors, and persistently overcome various difficulties in the entrepreneurial process to achieve innovation and business success.

The spirit of balancing righteousness and profit. Righteousness and profit represent two different value orientations pursued by businesses. Confucius believed, "The superior man understands what is right; the inferior man understands what will sell." Confucianism advocates sacrificing life for righteousness, which initiated the discourse on valuing righteousness over profit. China has always valued fairness and justice, believing that people should act selflessly like the heavens and the earth and that acting for legitimate interests constitutes a career, while acting for justice is considered virtuous. Xunzi considered vulgar people to regard wealth and profit as the highest standard, thus lacking the spirit of justice. Later, people gradually recognized the necessity and importance of balancing righteousness and profit, advocating mutual benefit for the world, benefiting the country, the people, and the world.

The spirit of honesty and trustworthiness. A person stands by credibility, a business thrives on credibility, and a country's prosperity depends on its credibility. Honesty and trustworthiness are the basic principles of being human and fundamental to conducting business. Integrity is the core of business ethics, the basic norm for maintaining business order, and is elevated to the principle of heaven, believing "If heaven acts without faith, it will not be able to cycle through the seasons; if the earth acts without faith, plants and trees will not grow." This means that the fundamental spirit of the heavenly way is to operate consistently according to objective laws without deviation, and people should emulate this characteristic of the heavenly way, being truthful and keeping promises, ensuring consistency between words and actions.

The spirit of harmonious coexistence. Traditional Chinese culture has always valued harmony as a prized goal and evaluation system. Harmonious coexistence is the essence of Chinese culture and an essential principle for managing relationships with nature, society, interpersonal relations, families, enterprises, businesses, ethnic groups, and nations. The business philosophy lies in "wealth comes from harmony," requiring unity and harmony within enterprises and symbiotic relationships among enterprises. As entrepreneurs seek business development, whether involving development dynamics, incentive mechanisms, external relations, or social responsibilities, they need to implement the value concept of harmonious culture.

However, as founding leader Chairman Mao Zedong said, traditional Chinese culture contains both "essence" and "dregs." Therefore, while leveraging the positive aspects of traditional Chinese culture to cultivate the entrepreneurial spirit, it is also necessary to guard against the negative influences of traditional culture. These negative influences may manifest as:

The concept of "a tall tree catches the wind" might discourage people from pursuing innovation excellence, settling for mediocrity, and lacking the courage to stand out and achieve great deeds;

The idea of "the victor becomes king, the loser becomes an outlaw" might make people fear failure, hesitate to take risks, and only judge heroes by success or failure, lacking the courage to persevere and turn failures into success;

The principle of "following rules strictly, not overstepping bounds" might lead people to stick to old ways, confining themselves to outdated modes of thinking and acting and lacking the courage to explore new methods, models, and paths.

These cultural factors could negatively impact the entrepreneurial spirit. In the context of economic globalization, it is necessary to organically integrate the positive elements contained in Chinese culture with the modern spirit. In the globalized economy, businesses face broader economic spaces, larger market sizes, more diversified market structures, and consumer demands. This environment requires entrepreneurs to adopt new spatial and speed concepts, market and consumption, production and supply, and resource and factor concepts. Entrepreneurs must be adept at optimizing the allocation of various resources and factors globally, and integrating markets and industrial chains globally to enhance the international competitiveness of enterprises.

(3) New Generation Entrepreneurs and Entrepreneurial Spirit

Mark Greeven, in his book "China's Disruptors," notes: "The era when all tech unicorns, digital disruptors, and well-known entrepreneurs came from Silicon Valley has long passed, and a new generation of Chinese entrepreneurs is rapidly taking the stage. Included are entrepreneurs who returned from studying abroad to establish many high-tech businesses and digital natives who have disrupted traditional industries—they tirelessly pursue rapid expansion with passion and fearlessness." In the tide of China's reform, opening up, and market economy, a group of outstanding entrepreneurs at the forefront has emerged, making significant contributions to China's economic development and the well-being of its people.

Looking at the entrepreneurial journey of these new entrepreneurs from the era of China's reform and opening up, we can see their characteristics of innovation and creativity, reflecting the essence of the spirit of new Chinese entrepreneurs:

- Market-oriented, pursuing development characteristics and spirit. The entrepreneurial environment for new Chinese entrepreneurs has shifted from a planned economy to a market economy. They are no longer business leaders who revolve around the government, asking for money and quotas under the planned system. They have become entrepreneurs who face the market, explore markets, and meet market demands. Outstanding entrepreneurs like Lu Guanqiu, Ren Zhengfei, and Li Shufu are private entrepreneurs who have grown in the ocean of the market economy, independent from the planned system, with their own property rights, management rights, and decision-making rights. They adapt to market changes and target market demands and center their entrepreneurship and management around customers.
- Technological innovation, pursuing breakthrough characteristics and spirit. Innovation is an essential driver of enterprise progress. New entrepreneurs have evolved from traditional enterprises that

relied solely on low costs and price advantages. They are committed to technological and organizational innovation, continually creating new products, processes, materials, markets, and organizational forms. Ren Zhengfei's team has "charged at a wall for decades," striving to acquire a technological system with independent intellectual property rights, obtaining over 120,000 effective authorized patents, and leading internationally in communications technology. Jack Ma's team was the first in China to establish an e-commerce platform, pioneering a new organizational sales mode while innovating in artificial intelligence, the Internet of Things, blockchain, and cloud computing to provide users with more intelligent, secure, and convenient e-commerce services.

- Refined management, pursuing excellence characteristics and spirit. Enterprise management is a critical way to improve efficiency. New entrepreneurs have evolved from extensive management styles and are committed to refining and modernizing management. By optimizing management, they save energy and human resources, reducing production costs, primarily through digital empowerment of enterprise management, continuously enhancing the modernization and efficiency levels of enterprise management. Under Zhang Ruimin's leadership, Haier Group achieved a smart transformation of management, with orderly processes from factories and workshops to the entire management chain, instantly accessing global user information and mobilizing global resources, significantly improving collaboration levels and efficiency, and through personalized services meeting consumers' diverse needs, winning more market for Haier products. Under Dong Mingzhu's leadership at Gree Group, particular attention is paid to detail management, focusing on cultivating good behavior and habits among employees and strictly enforcing various regulations and systems.
- Social dedication, pursuing harmony characteristics and spirit. Fulfilling social responsibility is an essential characteristic of contemporary entrepreneurs. They promote social prosperity by creating material wealth and advancing social progress by ensuring employee welfare and food safety. They also actively engage in public welfare, supporting the development of science, education, culture, and poverty relief, making outstanding contributions to social harmony. Cao Dewang, the founder of Fuyao Group, practices the ethical spirit of Confucian culture and has long been dedicated to charity with personal donations totaling over 8 billion

yuan, earning the "China Charity Award." Zong Qinghou, leading the Wahaha Group, adheres to the concept that running a business should benefit the general public, enthusiastically supports public welfare causes, becoming a model for donating to education and aiding the needy.

6.5 Conclusion

In the wave of economic globalization, businesses in any open country cannot stand aloof. They need to leverage globalization to access foreign resources and markets, thus earning the dividends of globalization. As a typical emerging major country, China's need for foreign resources, technology, capital, and markets has become ever more important; Chinese enterprises have rapidly grown under globalization, embarked on multinational operations, and spawned a group of enterprises with international competitiveness. While founding these enterprises, a batch of excellent entrepreneurs with outstanding qualities and a new entrepreneurial spirit have been nurtured.

Looking at the large Chinese enterprises that have entered the Fortune Global 500, they have become shining new stars among the world's large enterprises. In recent years, these listed enterprises have shown diversified trends in affiliation, industry distribution, increasing business revenue, and uneven average profits. Overall, the scale of Chinese enterprises has significantly grown, R&D investment has continuously increased, brand value has gradually risen, and the degree of internationalization has steadily advanced. However, facing the global slowdown in economic growth and insufficient consumer demand, the economic efficiency of large Chinese enterprises has slightly declined. Compared to world-class enterprises, China's leading enterprises still have some gaps, including the need for optimization in industrial structure, increase in R&D intensity, improvement in brand value, and expansion in internationalization, especially the need to enhance economic efficiency. By analyzing the difficulties and problems existing in large Chinese enterprises, optimizing the many factors affecting the development of large enterprises, and improving the internal and external development environment, large Chinese enterprises will enter a new realm.

The success of large Chinese enterprises follows a common entrepreneurial logic: relying on the vast domestic market to promote scale expansion and enhance innovation capabilities and relying on advanced technology to nurture large enterprises and explore large markets. Simply put, it is to grow and strengthen through the positive interaction between the market and technology. Specifically, there are mainly two types: The first type is represented by Huawei, showing a model driven by technology, which means planning independent R&D technology and products from the early stage of entrepreneurship, relying on advanced technology and competitive products to enter and expand the market. The result is that while core technology reaches the international forefront, the market share also ranks among the top in the world. The second type is represented by Xiaomi, showing a model driven by the market, that is, aiming at the vast consumer market for technology R&D and integration, developing and producing competitive new products, relying on market size advantage to develop new technology and new products continuously. The result is that while continuously discovering new needs and markets, the enterprise's new technologies and products emerge in an endless stream.

With the gradual increase of large enterprises in China, a group of outstanding entrepreneurs with global influence has emerged. They fulfill the function of realizing new combinations of production factors through entrepreneurship, significantly contributing to the economy's prosperity and social progress. These entrepreneurs exhibit some excellent qualities and spirits, forming the core content of the Chinese entrepreneurial spirit. The new entrepreneurial spirit inevitably reflects the influence of traditional Chinese culture, promoting the spirit of unyielding self-improvement, balancing righteousness and profit, honesty and trustworthiness, and harmonious coexistence. However, it also inevitably reflects the impact of the economy's market transformation and economic globalization, showing modern entrepreneurs' excellent qualities and spirit, including market-oriented pursuit of development, technological innovation for breakthroughs, refined management for excellence, and social contribution for harmony. These entrepreneurs' excellent qualities and spirit are rooted in a new era and new national conditions, becoming the essence of our times' spirit, forming positive factors that drive China's economic development and social progress.

References

Atkinson, R D., and Lind, M. (2018). *Big Is Beautiful: Debunking the Myth of Small Business*. Massachusetts, USAL: MIT Press.

Business School of Renmin University Website. (2023). Research on the Evaluation System of World-Class Enterprises. Available at: www.rmbs.ruc.edu.cn/xwzx/jsgd/79b98ff25381488cb0c71b73d261fd0d.htm [accessed May 21, 2024].

Chandler, A. D. (1990). *Scale and Scope: The Dynamics of Industrial Capitalism*. Massachusetts: Harvard University Press.

China Enterprise Confederation. (2019). *2019 China Top 500 Enterprises Development Report*. Beijing: Enterprise Management Press.

Cui, X., and Ouyang, H. (2020). Cultivating World-Class Enterprises with Global Competitiveness in China: Progress, Gap, and Strategy. *Economic Perspectives*, Vol. 5, pp. 28–40.

Dong, X. (2018). *The Revelation of Huawei: From Following to Leading*. Peking: Peking University Press.

Green, M. (2021). *Chinese-Style Innovation: The Business Model of New Innovative Enterprises*. Peking: CITIC Press.

Guangming Daily. (2019) *Chinese Innovation: From Catching Up to Leading*. Available at: https://news.gmw.cn/2017-07/30/content_25297946.htm [accessed May, 21, 2024].

Hebert, R F., and Link, A N. (2023). *A History of Entrepreneurship*. Guangxi Normal University Press.

Huawei. (2022). *Huawei Releases Its 2022 Annual Report: Operating Steadily, Continuing to Survive and Develop*. Available at: www.huawei.com/cn/news/2023/3/huawei-annual-report-2022 [accessed May 21, 2024].

Lei J. (2022). *Thoughts on Xiaomi's Entrepreneurship*. Peking: CITIC Press

Ouyang Y. (2024). *Development Economics of Large Countries*. Lausanne: Peter Lang Publishing.

Ouyang Y., Tang L. X. (2017). Innovation Path of Large Countries. *Economic Research Journal*, 52(9), 11–23.

Qin, T W. (2004). *Characteristics and Incubation Research of Entrepreneurial Spirit in the Era of Globalization*. Master's Thesis, Qingdao University.

Schumpeter, J. A., and Swedberg, R. (2021). The Theory of Economic Development. London: Routledge.

Tao, Y. (2020). *Huawei: From Made in China to Created in China*. Industry Press.

The 2005 List of the 25 Most Influential Business Leaders in China. Available at: *Fortune China* [accessed May 21, 2024].

The 2018 World's Top 500 Brands Announced. Available at: *China Daily* [accessed May 21, 2024].

The 2023 Fortune Global 500 Announced, Chinese Companies Lead the Global Tally. Available at: *Beijing Daily* [accessed May 21, 2024].

2023 Fortune Global 500 List Unveiled, Luxshare Precision Debuts. Available at: Sohu.com [accessed May 21, 2024].

The 2023 Top 500 Chinese Enterprises Revealed, Manufacturing Enterprises Increase for Three Consecutive Years. Available at: GMW.cn [accessed May 21, 2024].

The Development Journey of Xiaomi, Sohu.com, Xiaomi's Ten-Year Growth History. Available at: Sohu.com. [accessed May 21, 2024].

UN Trade and Development. (2019). *2019 World Investment Report*. Available at: https://unctad.org/publication/world-investment-report-2019 [accessed May 21, 2024].

Zhang, H L. (2017). *Huawei R&D*. Machinery Industry Press.

Zhang, H L. (2019). *Constructing Entrepreneurial Spirit from a Traditional Cultural Perspective*. Guangming Daily.

Zhang, K W. (2023). *How Far Are Chinese Enterprises from World-Class Enterprises*. The Paper.

Zhu, L. (2023). Entrepreneurial Spirit and Business Judgment from a Chinese Modernization Perspective: A Review and Outlook. *Journal of Shandong University of Finance and Economics*, 1, 36–43.

7 Entrepreneurship in Bangladesh

Md. Shajahan Kabir

7.1 Institutional Entrepreneurship in Developing Countries

The focus of scholarly discourse on institutional entrepreneurship has been on the actions of wealthy and influential players (DiMaggio, 1988). Social and economic resources are often concentrated in the hands of a small number of people in developing countries, and these individuals are not very interested in altering the institutional status quo. Considering this, how is institutional entrepreneurship feasible in this situation? Can driven actors with limited resources create new institutions or begin the process of transforming already-existing ones? We can answer these questions by combining concepts from several fields. While scholars of entrepreneurship have argued that entrepreneurship itself involves the "creation" of new opportunities through the recombination and transformation of existing resources (Baker and Nelson, 2005), institutional researchers have noted that actors without resources can use the existing institutions in unintended ways to create new ones by leveraging a wide network of actors (Campbell, 2004). Recently, both schools of thought have come to refer to the act of "making do" by repurposing available materials as "bricolage." In an effort to reconcile these differences, we specifically define bricolage as making do with the institutions and resources at hand. It is challenging to address the vast scope and interconnectedness of the social problems that many developing nations face due to their lack of resources and hazy institutional framework.

The importance of inter-organizational cooperation has been emphasized by researchers. This type of cooperation, however, necessitates a distributed agency platform, and in many of the world's least developed nations, these platforms—which are crucial institutions

DOI: 10.4324/9781003602378-11

for promoting development—are absent and thus create institutional voids, as this paper defines them. Consequently, it is critical to investigate how entrepreneurial actors initially enable cooperation.

7.2 Social Entrepreneurship

Sustainable businesses that blend "business principles with a passion for social impact" are referred to as social entrepreneurs (SEs) (Wolk, 2008). They use business concepts to maintain their operations while pursuing the primary organizational goal of creating social value (Weerawardena & Sullivan Mort, 2006). A set of standards was established by Dees (2001) to establish whether an individual's actions qualify as socially entrepreneurial: adopting a mission to create and sustain social value (rather than just private value); spotting and aggressively pursuing new opportunities to further that mission; participating in a process of continuous innovation, adaptation, and learning; acting fearlessly without being constrained by available resources; and demonstrating increased accountability for the results produced as well as to the constituencies they serve (Dees, 2001).

Social entrepreneurship is a relatively new phenomenon in the world and in Bangladesh. The notion of social entrepreneurship was first introduced by Bangladeshi professor Muhammad Yunus, who was awarded the Nobel Peace Prize. According to Austin, Stevenson, and Wei-Skillern (2006), "entrepreneurial activities with an embedded social purpose" is the standard definition of social entrepreneurship. These days, it's a significant global economic phenomenon (Mair & Marti, 2009a; Zahra et al. 2008). The implementation of new business models that address fundamental human needs, like the provision of inexpensive surgeries to cure blindness or the installation of sanitation systems in rural villages, is the source of some of the most impressive social entrepreneurship innovations that have come out of developing nations (Seelos & Mair, 2005; Elkington & Hartigan, 2008). It is a vast and varied movement for practical social change that uses cutting-edge business know-how and technological innovations to meet the needs of the underprivileged in a community. The practice of combining opportunity, inventiveness, and resourcefulness to address pressing social and environmental challenges is known as social entrepreneurship. The primary goal of social entrepreneurs is to change the systems and behaviors that underlie poverty, marginalization, environmental degradation, and the resulting erosion of human dignity. In the process, they might establish for-profit or nonprofit organizations, and, in both scenarios, bringing about sustainable system change is their main goal.

Social entrepreneurs are those who start social businesses. These are the people who have come up with creative answers to the most important social issues facing society. They are the driven and aspirational individuals who take on significant societal problems and present fresh concepts for comprehensive transformation. Instead of entrusting the government or commercial sectors to address societal needs, social entrepreneurs identify the issues and work to change the system, disseminate the solution, and inspire entire societies to make revolutionary changes. Social entrepreneurs are individuals or groups that use innovation in the economy and technology to further social objectives. Instead of pursuing profit, they use their entrepreneurial skills to start organizations that work toward a more equitable and compassionate society. Social entrepreneurship provides for the basic needs of the impoverished, including such as those described by the UN Millennium Development.

7.2.1 Importance of Social Entrepreneurship

Social entrepreneurs act as the change agents for society, taking advantage of opportunities that others miss, enhancing existing systems, developing fresh ideas, and coming up with solutions to improve society. As entrepreneurs transform the face of business, social entrepreneurs play a critical role in the economic and social development of a nation. A social entrepreneur finds novel solutions to societal issues and then widely applies them, in contrast to a business entrepreneur who may found whole new industries. While profit and return are the usual metrics used by business entrepreneurs to evaluate performance, social entrepreneurs also consider a positive return to society.

Typically promoting wide-ranging social, cultural, and environmental objectives, social entrepreneurship is frequently linked to the nonprofit and voluntary sectors (Thompson, 2002). Certain companies or other enterprises may occasionally take profit into account. Even though social entrepreneurs typically begin with modest, neighborhood-based initiatives, they frequently focus on issues like waste management, small-business creation, and water accesall of which have local manifestations but worldwide significance.

According to Zahra et al. (2008), social entrepreneurs can create new global industries and replicate their creative solutions in different regions of the world. The combination of the concepts of social aspect and entrepreneurship yields social entrepreneurs (Mair et al., 2006; Martin et al., 2007). The concurrent pursuit of economic, social, and environmental goals by enterprising ventures is another name for social entrepreneurship (Haugh, 2007). Accordingly, the creation of revenue through endeavors aimed at achieving social goals is known as social entrepreneurship (Boschee, 2001). According to Dees (2001), social entrepreneurship is frequently perceived as a hybrid that incorporates aspects of social sector organizations and commercial entrepreneurship.

Thus, "activities and processes to enhance social wealth" (Zahra et al., 2008) or "entrepreneurship with a social purpose" (Austin et al., 2006) have come to encompass a wide range of activities, and the concept of social entrepreneurship has grown to resemble a large tent (Martin et al., 2007). According to the survey, 25- to 34-year-olds had the highest rates of entrepreneurial activity across all geographic regions surveyed (Drayton, 2002). The degree to which an entrepreneurial endeavor prioritizes social and commercial objectives can also differ.

According to Dorado (2006), GEM displays four types of social entrepreneurship endeavors:

> (1) Overlapping social and commercial entrepreneurial activity: this occurs when an individual launches or manages an organization that is both social and commercial in nature; (2) Pure commercial entrepreneurial activity: this occurs when an individual launches or manages a commercial organization without any specific social goals; and (3) Pure social entrepreneurial activity: this occurs when an individual launches or manages a social organization without any commercial activities. And (4) Concurrent social and commercial entrepreneurship (i.e., an individual founding or managing a separate social organization in addition to a commercial one). As a result, social entrepreneurship has a significant impact on the economy by launching new sectors, approving fresh business concepts, and providing funding for issues that society has long overlooked.
>
> Dorado (2006)

The following areas benefit from social entrepreneurs (Elkington, & Hartigan, 2008): (i) The idea that becoming an entrepreneur is a good career choice and that it is a high-status or media-recognized career path, which varies across cultures and geographical areas. The Middle East and North Africa (MENA), sub-Saharan Africa, and Latin America/Caribbean regions scored highly for these attitudes, while the European Union (EU) scored lower. Two-thirds of the respondents consider entrepreneurship to be a high-status profession, while only half of the respondents thought it was a good career choice and received positive media attention.

7.2.2 Factors Influencing the Development of Social Entrepreneurship in Bangladesh

By raising the national standard of living, business can significantly alter a society. Nonetheless, certain domains are solely handled by commercial establishments. Social business can help with those. Because of this, social business entrepreneurship is crucial in today's developing nations where many people live in poverty. This business model is defined as non-loss and non-dividend, with the goal of solving societal issues. Since the businesses continually reinvest their profits back into the company to uphold societal values, it is financially self-sustaining. This company's primary goal is not just to make money but also to address social issues by producing.

By coming up with creative ways to improve social value and persistently seeking out new chances for social benefits rather than the creation of private wealth, it finds solutions to social problems. Social entrepreneurs are responsible to society and to themselves for carrying out their social missions and making prudent use of resources. They work in a variety of organizations, including big and small, new and old, religious and secular, non-profit and for-profit, etc., and they take inspiration from the best ideas in both business and nonprofit sectors. While social entrepreneurs consider a positive return to society, business entrepreneurs typically evaluate their success in terms of profit and return on investment. Social entrepreneurship is frequently linked to a nation's nonprofit and voluntary sectors of the economy.

Some businesses may occasionally take profit into account because they need to expand in order to continue offering more services to the public. The primary focus of social entrepreneurs is changing the systems and practices that underlie poverty, marginalization, environmental degradation, and the ensuing erosion of human dignity. They create for-profit or non-profit organizations in the process.

It is widely believed that the following factors affect the growth of social business entrepreneurship in Bangladesh: government tax exemption policy; issues caused by local agencies to obtain illegal funds for business site approval; political instability and preferences; lack of government financial support; intricate government bureaucracy; public opinion of social business initiatives; entrepreneurs' lack of knowledge and experience; and lack of expertise and experience on the part of the business owners, absence of support from incubator groups, etc. The projects also touch on non-profit objectives, creative ideas, social networks, social leadership, ethics, and social welfare and values.

7.2.3 The Factor of Social Entrepreneur Intention

The origins of social entrepreneurship can be traced to the growth of the private sector. Despite decades of collaborative efforts by the public, private, and nonprofit sectors to address social needs, gaps and inequalities persisted, particularly in less developed nations. One such country where the concept of contemporary social entrepreneurship first emerged is Bangladesh. Namely, professor and banker Muhammad Yunus came up with the idea of microloans for the underprivileged to help them start their businesses (Yunus et al. (2007). Yunus established the Grameen Bank to give the oppressed effective assistance. By making money from the interest that creditors pay, this organization reinterprets what constitutes a "non-profit" service. As per Brown and Wyatt's (2015) findings, by redefining the enterprise's mission and reevaluating value-creating logic, social enterprises offer a novel approach to enacting the desired change.

The first step in social entrepreneurship is to recognize a social opportunity. Subsequently, an enterprise model is formulated, implementation resources are gathered, the enterprise is spawned and grown, and eventually it reaches its destination. Although the industry is getting more attention because of the availability of capital, the development of a microfinance model, and an evolving government support system, a comparable body of scholarly literature has not yet emerged to assess or direct practice (Dichter et al. 2013). Namely, there is a lack of theoretical literature on the topic and disagreement over the precise definition of social entrepreneurship because it is considered as a byproduct of more general concepts of social innovation and entrepreneurship. Second, research on social entrepreneurship is divided between the seemingly contradictory criteria of significance and practicability, according to Mair and Martí (2006). In line with this, the definition of social entrepreneurship is one of the most important questions that will never be fully answered because, as many scholars have pointed out, all business is social in the sense that it adds value (Spear 2005). In addition, Dees (1998) provided an explanation of the role of the social entrepreneur in the advancement of society. In brief, this definition can be stated as follows: social entrepreneurs play the role of change agents in the social sector.

The current literature defines social entrepreneurship as a sequence of events that begin with a perceived social opportunity, transform it into an enterprise model, locate and secure the funding required to carry out the enterprise, establish and grow the enterprise, and offer additional opportunities after the enterprise's goal is accomplished. It can manifest itself in a variety of ways, including starting a business, expanding an organization, or joining forces with another company (Short et al. 2009). Research indicates that social entrepreneurship is a process that can add value through resource innovation (Shaw and Carter 2007). To accomplish their primary objectives, social enterprises investigate and seize opportunities that can create social value by fostering social change or meeting social needs (Prieto 2014).

7.2.4 Theoretical Background

In previous sections of this paper, researchers talked about the definition of social entrepreneurship and its rise in India. In this section, the authors discuss the current social entrepreneurial model and other important research studies related to social entrepreneurial intentions. The first attempt to develop a model that could depict the emergence of social entrepreneurial intention was made by Mair and Noboa (2006). They used individual variables to measure intentions and suggested in their model of social entrepreneurial intention that the desire to start a social enterprise stems from perceptions of desirability. It is affected by a cognitive-emotional construct that consists of empathy as an emotional factor and moral judgment as a cognitive factor. Enablers, on the other hand, are self-efficacy and social support, and they also have an impact on perceived feasibility (Mair and Martí 2006). Figure 7.1 shows the social entrepreneurial intention model developed

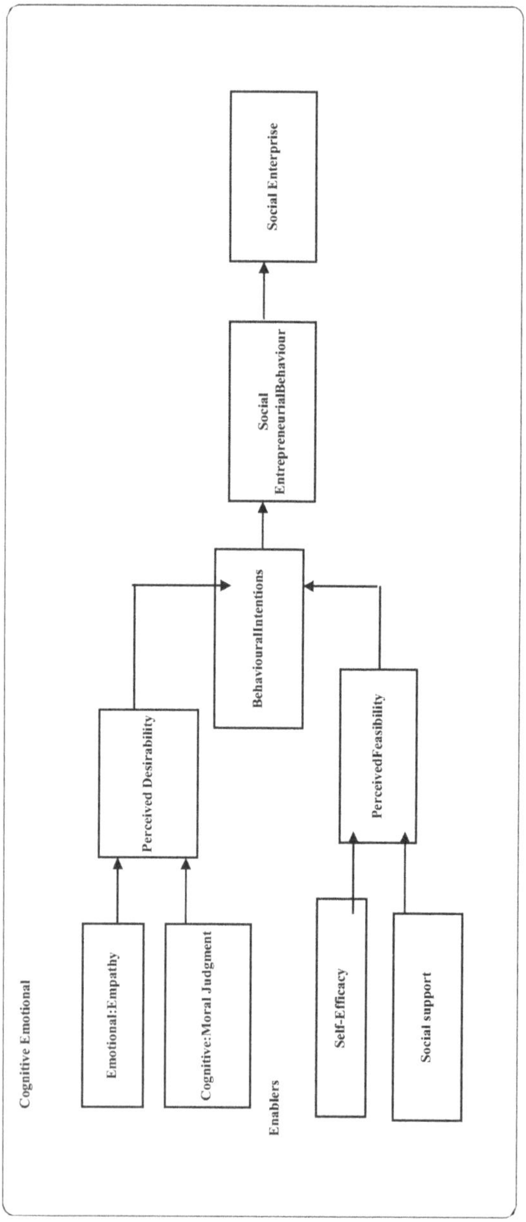

Figure 7.1 Social entrepreneurship intention, prepared according to Mair and Noboa's model.

Source: Mair and Noboa (2006).

by Mair and Noboa (2006). They added new components to Shapero's previously validated model (1982) of an entrepreneurial event. The model is distinct from traditional entrepreneurial models due to its antecedents of empathy and moral judgment. It remains an indisputable fact among researchers that individuals who exhibit moral discernment and empathy ultimately become social entrepreneurs.

However, moral judgment and empathy are necessary for the process of social entrepreneurial intention (Mair and Martí 2006). Researchers then tried to predict when social entrepreneurial intentions would emerge. In the paragraph that follows, we discuss intention studies conducted in the field of social entrepreneurship.

Kirby and Ibrahim (2011) carried out a study to ascertain the purpose of social entrepreneurial education in Egypt. The study's key finding is that researchers tried to find out how much knowledge Egyptian students had about social entrepreneurship to assist policymakers in encouraging students to pursue it as a career. The study's conclusions, which were based on a sample of 183 students, show that Egyptian students' knowledge of social entrepreneurship is insufficient and incomplete. Ernst (2011) carried out a follow-up study to determine the aspirations of 203 students from four different German universities to pursue social entrepreneurship. She made predictions about the intention to practice social entrepreneurship based on antecedents including age, gender, education, experience, personality traits, and role models. Variables extracted from the relationship between the effects of these antecedents was mediated by variables derived from the theory of planned behavior. Ernst (2011) was unable to find any evidence linking empathy and the intention of social entrepreneurship.

Mair and Noboa's (2006) model has been tried to be validated by Forster and Grichnik (2013). In their paper, they adapt the Mair and Noboa (2006) model and test its applicability with a sample of 159 corporate volunteers. They replaced perceived social support with the definition of collective efficacy, which they described as the type of environment and guiding organ.

Some researchers went on to create related models because of this. So, Hockerts (2015) attempted validation using the Mair and Noboa model. He changed the model by removing the mediating variables (perceived feasibility and desirability) in order to examine the direct effects of moral obligation, entrepreneurial self-efficacy, empathy, and perceived social support on social entrepreneurial intention.

He used three different samples for the study and found that there was a positive correlation between the sample and the intention to pursue social entrepreneurship (Hockerts 2015). Even though only a few studies have used empirical methods to investigate the influence of antecedents on social entrepreneurial intentions, these studies are essentially copies of each other.

Even though there are still a lot of unanswered questions about social entrepreneurship, management and academic institutions are becoming more and more interested in it. Thus, the purpose of this study is to go over the antecedents of some new social entrepreneurial intentions.

7.2.5 Social Entrepreneurship—"Hybrid Organizations"

Scholars understand what is known as "hybridity" (Evers & Laville 2005; Chew 2008: 23; Pache & Santos 2011). It is claimed that "hybrid organizations" combine and apply the logic of the theoretical categories of the market, the state, and civil society—which are typically viewed as three separate realms. Therefore, SE's significance for academic study goes beyond its presumed great social effect potential. Additionally, it has an impact on the widely accepted tri-sectoral model (Pestoff 1992). With all its dimensions, SE may supplement or add to already-existing charitable or public endeavors, or it may even partially replace or reshape them. The idea of "entrepreneurship" is shared by the two distinct characteristics of "Social Entrepreneurial Organizations" (SEOs), namely similarities to innovation and the promotion of social and institutional change.

To investigate this subject, it is required to outline and go over the entire spectrum of "entrepreneurship," including "economic entrepreneurship" and "non-economic entrepreneurship" (Skloot 2000).

Germany should be a model for developed nations for two main reasons: First of all, in a nation with a long history of a robust welfare state, it is astounding to see an increasing number of SEOs taking on social issues. Second, a sizable portion of multinational firms are actively pursuing it. This represents an additional aspect of the allure that social entrepreneurship holds in Germany and serves as a tangential link to the cultural perspective that the paper's five SEOs from Bangladesh and five SEOs from Germany provide as its main feature.

Being dubbed the "mother of social business" (Yunus & Weber, 2007), Bangladesh is largely reliant on the private sector and civil society for its social issue engagement. As a result, it can be considered a model for social entrepreneurship in developing nations and has been the focus of numerous academic studies in the past (Seelos & Mair 2005; Mair & Marti 2009b, for example).

These studies can be expanded upon by adding examples of social entrepreneurship.

7.2.6 Range of Social Entrepreneurship Derivation Strategies

As we've seen, SEOs exhibit key components of both economic and non-economic entrepreneurship as well as business principles, which can be summed up and condensed as follows: It can be argued that SEOs play a "vanguard role" because they frequently develop completely novel and unheard-of strategies or adapt and enhance already-existing strategies to address social issues in a novel way, as demonstrated by performance management initiatives. Since their actions are not primarily motivated by commercial objectives, we can observe that, in this instance, Schumpeter's definition of entrepreneurship includes an element of innovation that primarily relates to its non-economic form.

The same explains the SEOs' function as institutional entrepreneurs who, by acting to alter preexisting structures, also propel social change. The fact that most SEOs appear to be ahead of both societal attitudes and established frameworks emphasizes the SEO's role as "visionaries and strategists." Furthermore, in what both for-profit and nonprofit scholars refer to as a co-production process, the target groups are empowered and actively participate in finding a solution to the issue rather than gaining access to a service provided by others. While some SEOs still offer assistance, they don't concentrate on doing so freely; instead, they involve the target audience in the creation of added value.

In alternative models, the target audience directly generates the added value with SEO support. Partnership networks play a crucial role in helping SEOs to fortify their position and expand their influence through teamwork; in many cases, they are even required to establish the organization in the first place. A portion of the SEOs under study are in fact alliances between businesses that frequently come from different industries and have complementary skill sets. Other SEOs use collaborations for knowledge transfer, mutual learning, and discussion and exchange. Because SEOs must act as "politicians" when forming their crucial coalitions for partnerships, "social embeddedness" appears to be far more important to them than it is to commercial entrepreneurs. This goes beyond the innovation of entrepreneurial business models.

Considering that the SEO sociopolitical mission primarily necessitates a "grassroots" approach to gradually build up awareness, acceptability, trust, and credibility in direct interaction with the beneficiaries, the issue takes on even greater significance. In fields where personal delicacy is valued, as is likely the case with most social issues, this is a common occurrence where access from the top will not have the same impact, is impossible, or is being blocked. Additionally, as with end-user fees and corporate engagement, SEOs attempt to access a wide range of funding sources, of which governments and foundations are crucial components. It is frequently a case of outside participation that is essential for creating sustainable SEO models in the initial position. It is a hybrid of targeted for-profit fundraising initiatives and nonprofit fundraising strategies designed to increase revenue through fees.

But the combination is not the same as traditional commercial entrepreneurship. The most evident difference is arguably cross-subsidization, which results from the mission of social value creation being prevalent even for the "hard-to-serve." "Market orientation," which is represented by "customer orientation" and "competitor orientation," is also present in SE and is crucial to SEO success. However, because of the social component and the desire to work toward societal improvements, rivals may occasionally be viewed as allies or complements. In addition, there are still definite disparities with regard to business. Target audiences demand careful thought and specially designed "business models."

This is especially true when it comes to the frequently observed strong socio-political mission, which is seen as a characteristic of non-economic entrepreneurs. This, in turn, may contribute to the exceptionally strong cohesiveness that exists between the SEO and its clientele. Additionally, SEOs frequently appear to have a large clientele, which makes meeting their needs holistically more difficult than it would be for organizations with less hybrid structures. The effort to create a distinctive value proposition is another obvious feature, as the range of services and goods offered represents a sophisticated and extremely qualitative combination of features that produce a fit that is very difficult to replicate.

The specifics of the SE concept that were just discussed and are shared by industrialized and developing nations alike raise hopes that SEOs can address or at least lessen two specific flaws in the voluntary sector that Anheier (2005: 130 p.) identified. We call the first one "philanthropic insufficiency." The phrase implies that the relative charity of a small number of people will not be adequate to address the wide range of needs in contemporary society. However, it draws attention to the fact that volunteer labor contributes significantly to human resources in nonprofit organizations. While volunteerism is a good way to get involved in the community, it can also result in a shortage of highly qualified, experienced staff. Anheier (2005) goes on to describe governments as balancing partners who help nonprofits overcome their shortcomings. He refers to the greater resources available to governments as well as the potential for raising standards and benchmarks to improve quality in the nonprofit sector.

Teams may become more professional because of SEOs' growing business acumen and entrepreneurial practices. Increased productivity and first-rate efficacy could make expert compensation simpler and draw experts to work as SEOs. This very feature might also greatly expand the reach of social impact initiatives and solve the issue of "philanthropic insufficiency." Organizations could achieve this goal even if they are still reliant on government or charitable funding by using their resources more wisely and creatively or by creating new services or goods.

Furthermore, it is highly unlikely that governments could make up for the nonprofit sector's current shortcomings given the financial difficulties faced by practically every welfare state and the unique difficulties faced by developing nations, such as extreme welfare disparities or corruption. In any event, SEOs appear to be a useful addition to the range of nonprofit and governmental social impact activity providers currently available. But we must remember that there are always losers in markets.

*7.2.7 **Social Entrepreneurship Initiatives in Bangladesh***

- BRAC

Fazle Hasan Abed founded BRAC in 1972 as a small-scale relief and rehabilitation initiative to try to make up for some of the destruction brought about by Bangladesh's liberation war. But by 1974, a plethora of social issues forced BRAC to embrace a new integrated development strategy centered on the dual goals of empowering the poor and reducing poverty, with an emphasis on institutional development to integrate the impoverished in rural areas into the mainstream of development. Thirty years later, BRAC employed over 93,000 people and its reach extended to 78% of the country's villages, making it the second largest employer in the country after the government.

By offering microcredit and encouraging impoverished rural residents to become self-sufficient, BRAC has the potential to integrate the impoverished into the mainstream of development. To date, the organization has served over five million impoverished and landless individuals, the majority of whom are women. In addition, it promotes social welfare by growing its core programs, which now cover four fundamental areas: economic development, health, education, and social development, as well as human rights and legal services. Fazle Hasan Abed, a crucial member of BRAC, possesses exceptional leadership qualities to spearhead the strategy for the nation's poorest citizens' development. Success in social entrepreneurship requires a combination of knowledge, skill, and experience. Fazle Hasan Abed's knowledge enabled him to guide the plan in the right direction, and his skill and experience allowed him to make better decisions for the entrepreneurship program. In the social business sector, social entrepreneurs often have to deal with risk and uncertainty. For example, their policies may conflict with governmental policies or cultural norms, or they may fail to establish themselves as a hub for the impoverished. The capacity and desire to engage in some form of social welfare is a crucial component of social entrepreneurship success.

- ASA

In its early years, ASA ran several development initiatives, including educating the public about social action, preparing local birth attendants, and strengthening journalistic capacity, among other things. It started implementing new initiatives in the mid-1980s that focused on education, sanitation, health and nutrition, and other areas. At this point, ASA launched microcredit as a test project. Based on its practical experience in the field and analysis of the effects of development assistance, ASA concluded that the impoverished require financial stability in order to make significant improvements in their lives. This change in perspective caused ASA to concentrate only on microfinance as a means of combating poverty in 1992. ASA sought to change its business practices so that it could become independent and stop depending on ASA's Microfinance Model. ASA steadily changed to become the well-known "ASA Cost-effective and Sustainable Microfinance Model" thanks to donor funding and grants.

By using this model, ASA quickly achieved self-sufficiency and in 2001 proclaimed itself to be a "donor free MFI." Within a year, a branch has become self-sufficient thanks to this model, which ASA has tested and refined in the field. Any MFI that implements this model for operations quickly reaches sustainability. Many MFIs worldwide have embraced it to achieve results as quickly as possible. By the end of December 2011, ASA had opened 3,154 branches, effectively expanding its reach throughout Bangladesh. Its 21,422 employees are working nonstop to provide services to over 4.94 million customers. As a nonprofit, ASA understood the role that microfinance played in addressing the dearth of access to capital for the underprivileged community. ASA works to promote self-reliance among the impoverished by reaching out to the marginalized, empowering women, and strengthening the ability of small groups of people to take charge of their own lives. The ASA's Microfinance Model underwent a gradual transformation into the well-known "ASA Cost-effective and Sustainable Microfinance Model" on a global scale. Since its founding in 1978, ASA has dedicated itself to helping the underprivileged and has worked to establish social welfare and values through an effective Microfinance Institution (MFI).

• The Grameen Bank

Muhammad Yunus, the creator, and manager of Grameen Bank, which was founded in 1983, and its expanding network of social venture companies, is one well-known example of a modern social entrepreneur. The work of Yunus and Grameen is consistent with a current trend in social entrepreneurship, which highlights the tremendous advantages and synergies that arise from combining business concepts with social endeavors. He found that traditional banks would not give loans without collateral, even though entrepreneurship was by no means an uncommon trait among the impoverished. Currently, Grameen Bank provides loans to over 7.5 million impoverished individuals—of whom 97% are women—helping them overcome their circumstances. Sixty-eight percent of the families that borrow money from Grameen Bank have left poverty behind. The idea of "social business," which is still in the process of development, emerged from the Grameen Group's nearly three decades of experience creating businesses aimed at reducing poverty (Henton et al., 1997). Grameen Bank serves 79,152 villages through the assistance of its 2452 branches, which accounts for more than 94% of all villages in Bangladesh. This bank has a higher loan recovery rate than any other banking system, at 98%.

7.3 Conclusion

According to this study, Bangladesh has a thriving social enterprise sector where women and young people are overrepresented compared to traditional businesses. Most social entrepreneurs anticipate having more employees and higher employee turnovers in the next year. Social enterprises are creating jobs.

Social entrepreneurship and its protagonists, the "unreasonable" social entrepreneurs, have been introduced as a phenomenon that provides innovative solutions to the world's most pressing problems, such as poverty, health, education, unemployment, social integration, and the environment. This chapter aspires to contribute to the advancement of the phenomenon through research efforts analyzing the role of social entrepreneurial organizations in public goods provision and their strategies to fulfil this role. Social entrepreneurship generates social innovation and change by leveraging their organization's capacity to address social issues profitably. They are characterized by a mindset to strive for social value creation in a way that is attractive to business They pursue societal value creation in a persistent, learning, and outreaching manner and apply the skills of entrepreneurship and communication. Social entrepreneurship collaborates with NGOs to generate societal impact and obtain missing knowledge and skills at business schools. Corporations interested in social entrepreneurship should be thinking of providing a supportive environment in which social entrepreneurship can develop and test their ideas. Crucial for their success is senior management sponsorship, an understanding of how business and society can be bought together, and the creation of space for experimentation. NGOs and development organizations are invited to explore their membership rosters for potential social entrepreneurship to leverage corporate activities to the benefit of society. Likewise, business schools have a role to play in inspiring and training social entrepreneurship, especially developing the entrepreneurial as well as communication skills needed to succeed. In general, the phenomenon of social entrepreneurship might be a visible sign of people looking for ways to reconcile their social and working lives.

Scientifically, social entrepreneurship is a new, interdisciplinary research field lacking a general definition. To create a working definition for social entrepreneurship, the constitutive terms of the phenomenon were analyzed. Entrepreneurship itself is an interdisciplinary phenomenon that lacks an agreed definition and thus was shaped by several contributors, such as Say, Schumpeter, Kirzner, Drucker, and Stevenson, who each added defining dimensions of entrepreneurship from their perspective. Opportunity recognition, innovation and transformation, organization, leadership and management, and the personal qualities of the entrepreneur emerged as the defining characteristics of entrepreneurship, but the degree of certain characteristics is still under discussion.

Youth social entrepreneurship has the potential to mobilize young people as agents of change. Youth social entrepreneurship represents an inclusive form of development in that it both empowers youth through employment and leverages their talents and capacities in the service of social good. It can contribute directly to achieving Sustainable Development Goal 8 through employment creation and indirectly to achieving several other Goals through its social impact mission.

The other common element is that policies and interventions must be based on evidence. The collection and analysis of relevant data are essential for ensuring that youth social entrepreneurship ecosystems effectively respond to the real needs of young people and propel them towards their full agency as social entrepreneurs supporting the achievement of the 2030 Agenda for Sustainable Development.

Bangladesh's social entrepreneurship sector is an emerging and competitive sector of the economy and accounts for a substantial portion of the country's GDP. It not only helps vulnerable communities by empowering them, creating jobs, and addressing social exclusion across the nation but it also boosts productivity, resulting in huge profits and a growing economy.

Since BRAC primarily operates in Bangladesh's rural areas, our goal in this section is to briefly highlight some of the most significant obstacles that many rural residents must overcome in order to engage in public life and markets. The asymmetrical relationships between various community members—elites at one extreme and the helpless at the other—are a defining feature of Bangladesh's rural areas. The local elites are able to increase their control over both public and private land, local government resources (such as capital, government agricultural land, health infrastructure, and government primary schools), and who is employed in specific jobs (e.g., by bribery, manipulation, or prestige) through a variety of mechanisms.

They also use their ability to control liquid capital by charging exorbitant interest rates on loans. In this situation, the helpless impoverished rely heavily on their capacity to secure the backing of the local upper class to survive. Usually, receiving this support means giving up their freedom and independence. To finance bribes to obtain jobs, for example, many sell their land. Those with nothing to contribute to the elite are shut out of these "dependent security" relationships. Development experts point out that poverty has many facets, including injustice, powerlessness, and gender inequality in addition to material poverty. Bangladesh's official legal system is thought to be exceedingly slow and corrupt (Transparency International of Bangladesh, 2005; 2018).

Because they cannot afford to pay bribes or wait interminably for dispute settlements, the majority of impoverished people are unable to rely on the formal system. Therefore, because of its lower cost, speed, accessibility, and cultural relevance, the informal legal system is typically preferred. But because of its high levels of corruption and dominance by the male elite, both formal and informal systems are employed to maintain power dynamics. The ideological framework of customs, norms, and values interacts with the power structure and is strengthened by it. Within Bangladesh's rural communities, women are the most impoverished group, experiencing extreme poverty. Women's freedom is restricted by social and cultural norms related to patriarchy, purdah, and the still-highly prevalent practice of early marriage. The prevalence of early marriages and patriarchy impose restrictions on women's mobility and participation in public life. Women are restricted to the private sphere by a rigid division between the public and private domains, which limits their ability to engage in market exchanges and income-generating activities.

Another problem relates to resource ownership: despite women's ability to own resources, men are still expected to control them due to societal norms. Because of this, many mainstream development initiatives aimed at empowering women (such as microfinance) pass over the intended beneficiaries—women and girls—in favor of recipients who are more culturally acceptable—men and boys. As a result, resource availability does not always translate into resource utilization. All things considered, the intricate power structure of rural

Bangladesh, which is rooted in symbiotic relationships and sustained by prevailing sociocultural norms, combined with the frailty and corruption of the political and legal systems, limits the ability of the poor and helpless to participate in market-oriented endeavors.

The economy of a country influences the country's overall development and therefore, it is imperative that this sector gets as much support as it can from the Bangladeshi government. In this way, they will continue to contribute to the economy while also assisting disadvantaged communities by creating creative solutions to society's unresolved problems. It is also important for social enterprises to understand the market in order to provide innovative products demanded by people at the cheapest possible cost only then they will survive in the dynamic and competitive business environment of Bangladesh.

References

Anheier, H. K. (2005). *Nonprofit Organizations: Theory, Management, Policy*. London: Routledge.

Austin, J., Stevenson, H., and Wei-Skillern, J. (2006). Social and Commercial Entrepreneurship: Same, Different, or Both? *Entrepreneurship: Theory & Practice*, Vol. 30, No. 1, pp. 1–22.

Baker, T., and Nelson, R.E. (2005), "Creating Something from Nothing: Resource Construction through Entrepreneurial Bricolage", *Administrative Science Quarterly*, Vol. 50, pp. 329–66

Boschee, J. (2001). *The Social Enterprise Sourcebook*. Minneapolis, MN: Northland Institute.

Brown, T., and Wyatt, J. (2015). Design Thinking for Social Innovation. *Annual Review of Policy Design*, Vol. 3, No. 1, pp. 1–10.

Campbell, J.L. (2004), *Institutional Change and Globalization*. Princeton, NJ: Princeton University Press.

Chew, C. (2008). *Social Enterprises in Disguise? Towards Hybrid Forms of Voluntary and Charitable Organizations in the UK*. Research Working Paper RP08/49. Aston University, Birmingham.

Dees, J. G. (1998), Enterprising Non-profits, *Harvard Business Review* 76(1), 55–67

Dees, J. G. (2001). The Meaning of Social Entrepreneurship. Retrieved May 3, 2009, from www.caseatduke.org/documents/dees_sedef.pdf

Dichter, S., Katz, R., Koh, H., and Karamchandani, A. (2013). Closing the pioneer gap. *Stanford Social Innovation Review*, Vol. *11*, No. 1, pp. 36–43.

DiMaggio, J. (1988), Interest and Agency in Institutional Theory", in Zucker, L.G. (ed.), *Institutional Patterns and Organizations: Culture and Environment*. Cambridge, MA: Ballinger, pp. 3–22.

Doherty, B., Haugh, H., and Lyon, F. (2014). Social Enterprises as Hybrid Organizations: A Review and Research Agenda. *International Journal of Management Reviews*,Vol. *16*, No. 4, pp. 417–436.

Dorado, S. (2006). Social Entrepreneurial Ventures: Different Values so Different Process of Creation, No? *Journal of Developmental Entrepreneurship*, Vol. 11, No. 4, pp. 319–343.

Drayton, W. (2002). The Citizen Sector: Becoming as Entrepreneurial and Competitive as Business. *California Management Review*, Vol. 44, No. 3, pp. 120–132

Elkington, J., and Hartigan, P. (2008). *The Power of Unreasonable People: How Social Entrepreneurs Create Markets that Change the World.* Boston, MA: Harvard Business Press.

Ernst, K. K. (2011). Heart Over Mind – An Empirical Analysis of Social Entrepreneurial Intention Formation on the Basis of the Theory of Planned Behaviour. Ph.D. Thesis, University of Wuppertal.

Evers, A., and Laville, J.L. (2005). Social Services by Social Enterprises: On the Possible Contributions of Hybrid Organizations and a Civil Society. In Evers, A. and Laville, J.L. (eds.), *The Third Sector in Europe*. Cheltenham: Edward Elgar, pp. 237–256.

Forster, F., and Grichnik, D. (2013). Social Entrepreneurial Intention Formation of Corporate Volunteers. *Journal of Social Entrepreneurship*, Vol. 4, No. 2, pp. 153–181 http://doi.org/10.1080/19420676.2013.777358.

Haugh, H. (2007). New Strategies for a Sustainable Society: The Growing Contribution of Social Entrepreneurship. *Business Ethics Quarterly*, Vol. 17, No. 4, pp. 743–749.

Henton, Douglas, John, M., and Kimberly W. (1997). *Grassroots Leaders for a New Economy* . San Francisco: Jossey-Bass.

Hockerts, K. (2015). The Social Entrepreneurial Antecedents Scale (SEAS): A Validation Study. *Social Enterprise Journal*, Vol. 11, No. 3, pp. 260–280. http://doi.org/10.1108/SEJ-05-2014-0026.

Kirby, D. A., and Ibrahim, N. (2011). The Case for (Social) Entrepreneurship Education in Egyptian Universities. *Education + Training*, Vol. *53*, No. 5, pp. 403–415. http://doi.org/10.1108/00400911111147712.

Mair, J., and Martin, I. (2009a). Entrepreneurship in and around Institutional Voids: A Case Study from Bangladesh. *Journal of Business Venturing*, Vol. 24, pp. 419–435.

Mair, J., and Maritn, I. (2009b). Social Entrepreneurship as Institution Building. In Robinson, J. A., Mair, J. and Hockerts, K. (eds.), *International Perspectives on Social Entrepreneurship*. Basingstoke, Hampshire: Palgrave Macmillan, pp. 144–160.

Mair, J., and Martí, I. (2006). Social Entrepreneurship Research: A Source of Explanation, Prediction, and Delight. *Journal of World Business*, Vol. *41*, No. 1, pp. 36–44. http://doi.org/10.1016/j.jwb.2005.09.002.

Mair, J., and Noboa, E. (2006). Social Entrepreneurship: How Intentions to Create a Social Venture Are Formed. In *Social Entrepreneurship*. UK: Palgrave Macmillan, pp. 121–135.

Mair, J., Robinson, J., and Hockerts, K. (2006). *Social Entrepreneurship*. New York: Palgrave MacMillan. http://doi.org/10.1057/ 9780230625655.

Martin, R. L., and Osberg, S. (2007). Social Entrepreneurship: The Case for Definition. *Stanford Social Innovation Review*, Vol. 5, No. 2, pp. 28–39.

Pache, A.-C. and Santos, F. (2011). *Inside the Hybrid Organization: An Organizational Level View of Responses to Conflicting Institutional Demands. Working Paper 11001*. ESSEC Business School, Cergy Pontoise.

Pestoff, V. (1992). Third Sector and Co-Operative Services – An Alternative to Privatization. *Journal of Consumer Policy*, Vol. 15, No. 1, pp. 21–45.

Prieto, L. C. (2014). Is Wal-Mart a Social Enterprise? An Exploration of the Relationship between Corporate Reputation, Corporate Social Responsibility & Financial Performance. *Academy of Strategic Management Journal,* Vol. 13, No. 2, pp. 51–61.

Schumpeter, J.A. (1934). *The Theory of Economic Development: An Inquiry into Profits, Capital, Credit, Interest, and the Business Cycle.* Cambridge, MA: Harvard University Press.

Seelos, C., and Mair, J. (2005). Social Entrepreneurship: Creating New Business Models to Serve the Poor. *Business Horizons*, Vol. 48, pp. 241–246. http://doi.org/10.1016/j.bushor.2004.11.006.

Shapero, A., and Sokol, L. (1982). The Social Dimensions of Entrepreneurship. In C. Kent, D. Sexton, & K. Vesper (Eds.), *Encyclopedia of Entrepreneurship* (pp. 72-90). Englewood Cliffs, NJ: Prentice-Hall.

Shaw, E., and Carter, S. (2007). Social Entrepreneurship. *Journal of Small Business and Enterprise Development*, Vol. 14, No. 3, pp. 418–434. http://doi.org/10.1108/14626000710773529.

Short, J. C., Moss, T. W., and Lumpkin, G. T. (2009). Research in Social Entrepreneurship: Past Contributions and Future Opportunities. *Strategic Entrepreneurship Journal*, Vol. 3, pp. 161–194. http://doi.org/10.1002/sej.

Skloot, E. (2000). Evolution or Extinction: A Strategy for Nonprofits in the Marketplace. *Nonprofit and Voluntary Sector Quarterly*, Vol. 29, pp. 315–324.

Spear, R. (2005). Social Enterprise for Work Integration in 12 European Countries: A Descriptive Analysis. *Annals of Public and Cooperative Economics*, Vol. 76, No. 2, pp. 195–231.

Thompson, J.L. (2002). The World of the Social Entrepreneur. *International Journal of Public Sector Management*, Vol. 15, No. 4/5, p. 413.

Transparency International (2018). Uganda Tops East Africa in Corruption. February.

Transparency International of Bangladesh (2005). *Corruption in Bangladesh: A Household Survey*, available at: www.ti-bangladesh.org/ (accessed January 2024).

Weerawardena, J., and Mort, G. S. (2006). Investigating Social Entrepreneurship: A Multidimensional Model. *Journal of World Business*, Vol. 41, pp. 21–35.

Wolk, A. M. (2008). *Advancing Social Entrepreneurship: Recommendations for Policy Makers and Government Agencies*. The Aspen Institute.

Yunus, M. & Weber, K. (2007). *Creating a World without Poverty: Social Business and the Future of Capitalism*. New York: Perseus Books.

Zahra, S. A., Gedajlovic, E., Neubaum, D.O., and Shulman, J.M. (2008). A Typology of Social Entrepreneurs: Motives, Search Processes and Ethical Challenges. *Journal of Business Venturing*, Vol. 24, pp. 519–532.

8 Entrepreneurships in Japan

An Overview

Mirjana Radović-Marković

8.1 Introduction

Population is important in determining the size of a given country. However, for further analysis that includes the most important indicators of economic growth and inclusion in global flows, size is not the only important issue. Namely, the structure of the population is also an important factor. Japan is the country with the fastest aging population in the world. As of 2023, more than 1 in 10 people in Japan are now aged 80 or older, and almost a third of its population is over 65—an estimated 36.23 million (WEF, 2023). This aging population is having a profound impact on Japan's economy, workforce, and society. In line with this, the aging of the population has recently been the main subject of experts' attention, as has the decline in fertility (ICGI, 1996). The decline in fertility can be explained by the fact that women in Japan are not ready to give birth and raise children alone due to the traditional model of upbringing. In addition, girls do not marry as quickly as their mothers' generations, so they give birth to children later. In addition, women's careers and business success have become increasingly important. The postponement of marriages also means the retardation of childbirth.

Based on a survey conducted in 2022, about 6.1% of respondents between the ages of 18 and 34 in Japan said they were in the process of starting their own business (Satoshi,2022). This is an extremely small percentage and creates fear among experts for the future of entrepreneurship development in this country. Namely, there is concern that an aging population could lead to a loss of entrepreneurial spirit (Ruiu and Breschi, 2019). However, it is important to note that this is not entirely true, given that many older individuals can contribute

DOI: 10.4324/9781003602378-12

significantly to entrepreneurial activities. In fact, seniors make up a third of all entrepreneurs in Japan (SilverEco, 2016).

8.2 Entrepreneurial Environment

The business environment of any organization includes competitive, cultural, demographic, economic, natural, political, regulatory, and technological factors (called environmental factors) that effect the operations, and growth of an organization. According to some recent research, the number of entrepreneurship universities in Japan that are ranked high in the world is increasing. For instance, the University of Tokyo is ranked 41st in Asia and 510th in the world for entrepreneurship (EduRank, 2024). At the same time, the number of entrepreneurs is decreasing. Thus, according to the list published by Approved Index, Japan is ranked as the country with the fourth least entrepreneurship in the world (Chattergoon, 2018). Therefore, many scientists who deal with this field rightly wonder where the entrepreneurs have disappeared and why the interest in performing entrepreneurial activities has decreased. Many experts look for the reason for such a situation in the fact that the status of entrepreneurs in Japan is not high and that society's perception of entrepreneurs is neutral. Therefore, "the typical Japanese parent often does not support his or her child's aspiration to become an entrepreneur." Instead, they choose an elite public university for their children, in order to get a job in a big company like Mitsubishi or Mitsui after they graduate. A well-known public company, such as Toyota or Hitachi, is also sufficient. Because of historical patterns of lifelong employment (shushin koyo), the vast majority of parents still believe that these paths represent the most stable careers, the highest cumulative pay, and the most prestige.

In the last ten years, Japan faces several challenges that impact its entrepreneurial climate. These include not only an aging population, but a strong yen, and a relatively inhospitable climate for startups. In this context, a report done by the Ministry of Economy, Trade and Industry showed that the number of new businesses in Japan increased by 4.5% in 2020, with a significant portion of these being digital startups (Asian Development Outlook, 2020). The report also highlights the importance of digital transformation for small and medium-sized enterprises (SMEs) in Japan, which can help them to improve their competitiveness and resilience. This concept of continuous improvement, known as "kaizen," is deeply ingrained in Japanese business culture (Wright, 2022). This philosophy encourages incremental changes and problem-solving at all levels of the organization, leading to enhanced resilience and adaptability

The Global Entrepreneurship Monitor (2022) provides a detailed view of the entrepreneurial landscape in Japan, including data on entrepreneurial behavior and attitudes, activity, motivations, impact, and societal values (GEM, 2022). This data can provide insights into the growth and challenges of entrepreneurship in Japan. It's important to note that while the growth is promising, the startup culture in Japan is still developing and there are various factors influencing its progress.

According to the Global Entrepreneurship Monitor (2024) report, the quality of the overall entrepreneurial environment in Japan declined sharply in 2023. While in 2022, the quality of the overall entrepreneurial environment in Japan was rated 5.0, ranking Japan 21st out of 50 countries, in 2023, this score dropped to 4.4, placing Japan in 27th position out of 49 countries (GEM, 2024).

Traditional Japanese corporations are increasingly looking to collaborate with startups or establish their own innovation labs to stay competitive in the rapidly evolving tech landscape. Investments into startups can come from various sources and can be facilitated through different methods. Here are some ways people invest in startups (Figure 8.1):

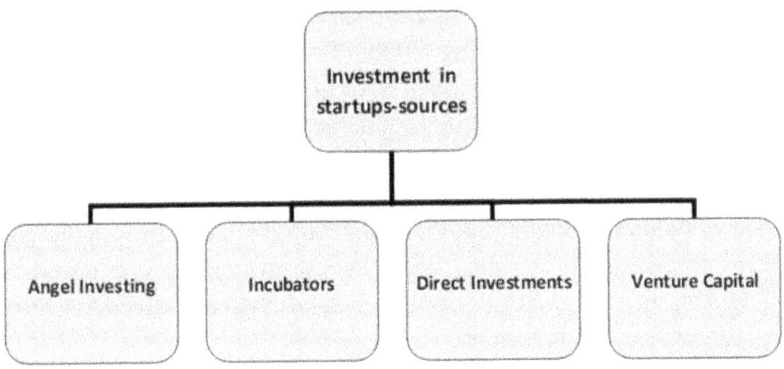

Figure 8.1 Sources of investment in startups.

Source: Author.

We will briefly explain the listed sources of startup investment:

- ✓ Angel Investing is a form of early-stage investment where affluent individuals provide capital to startups in exchange for equity.
- ✓ Incubators provide startups with mentorship, office space, and sometimes funding.
- ✓ Some investors might choose to directly invest in a startup
- ✓ Venture capitalists invest in startups and early-stage companies that have a potential for high growth.

This trend of investment has led to more partnerships, and acquisition opportunities for startups. There are over 10,000 startups in Japan, making new challenges every day (J-Startup, n.d.). However, companies that are active globally are still part of the minority. Namely, while Japan is known for its adherence to tradition, it also has a history of innovation and adaptation. Entrepreneurs in Japan often blend traditional values with modern technologies and business practices to create innovative products and services. In line with this, it can be concluded that despite these challenges, there are encouraging signs.

Given the sophistication of Japan's technological base, the promise of female entrepreneurs, the advent of startup incubators, and the rise of "intra-preneurship" within established companies, there are opportunities for growth.

"The outbreak of COVID-19 for many companies was a chance to reconsider employee relations and to adapt and change their corporate culture for mutual benefit" (Radović-Marković et al., 2021, p.6). Some research shows that about 88% of Japanese largest 6 corporations adopted remote work during 2020 (The Straits Times, 2022). In Japan, companies such as Fujitsu, Hitachi and Ricoh, the construction materials group Likil, the glass manufacturer AGC and others have accepted remote work as the "new normal," expecting it to continue this way after the pandemic ((Radović-Marković et al., 2021, p.7).

In conclusion, while tradition and culture can pose challenges to entrepreneurship in Japan, they also shape unique opportunities. Understanding these cultural nuances is crucial for fostering a more entrepreneurial environment.

8.3 Women Entrepreneurship in Japan

Women entrepreneurship in Japan has been steadily increasing in recent years, although the country still faces challenges in achieving gender parity in the business world. Historically, Japan has had a predominantly male-dominated business culture, with societal norms often favoring traditional gender roles. However, there has been a growing recognition of the importance of women's participation in the economy, leading to various initiatives and programs aimed at supporting female entrepreneurs. The position of women-owned firms in Japan during and after COVID-19 reflects a mix of challenges, resilience, and opportunities (Radović Marković, 2022). Despite facing challenges, many women-owned firms demonstrated resilience and innovation by adapting their business models, exploring new revenue streams, and leveraging technology to maintain operations and reach customers.

The Japanese government has implemented policies and programs to promote women's entrepreneurship as part of broader efforts to stimulate economic growth and address demographic challenges, such as the aging population and declining birth rates. These policies include financial incentives, tax breaks, and initiatives to encourage companies to hire and promote women into leadership positions. Despite these efforts, several challenges persist for women entrepreneurs in Japan, such as the following:

1. ***Cultural Biases***: Traditional gender roles and societal expectations often place women in caregiving roles, which can hinder their ability to pursue entrepreneurial ventures. Cultural biases may also lead to discrimination and stereotypes that undermine women's credibility and capabilities as business leaders.
2. ***Limited Access to Funding***: Women entrepreneurs in Japan often face difficulties accessing funding and venture capital compared to their male counterparts. This can be attributed to various factors, including biases among investors, risk aversion, and a lack of awareness about investment opportunities in women-led businesses.
3. ***Work-Life Balance***: Balancing work and family responsibilities can be particularly challenging for women in Japan, where traditional gender roles often place a significant emphasis on family duties. This can make it difficult for women entrepreneurs to dedicate the time and energy needed to grow their businesses while fulfilling societal expectations regarding caregiving and household duties.
4. ***Lack of Networking Opportunities***: Networking plays a crucial role in entrepreneurship, yet women in Japan may face barriers

to accessing professional networks and mentorship opportunities, which are often dominated by men. This lack of networking opportunities can limit women's access to the valuable resources, support, and guidance needed to succeed in business.

5. ***Underrepresentation in Leadership Positions***: Women are underrepresented in leadership positions in Japanese companies, which can indirectly impact their ability to pursue entrepreneurial ventures. The lack of female role models and mentors in business leadership positions may discourage women from taking entrepreneurial risks and pursuing ambitious career paths.
6. ***Gender Bias in Business Practices***: Gender bias in business practices, such as hiring and promotion decisions, can create additional challenges for women entrepreneurs. Discriminatory practices may limit women's access to key resources, opportunities for advancement, and support networks within the business community.

There are numerous success stories of women entrepreneurs in Japan who have overcome obstacles and achieved remarkable success in various industries, including technology, fashion, food, and services. The rise of successful female entrepreneurs in Japan has produced many benefits for the country, including economic growth, diversity and inclusion, and providing role models for young girls. Their success not only contributes to the economy but also serves as inspiration for other aspiring female entrepreneurs (ItsJapanese Team, 2024).

Addressing gender disparities, providing targeted support for women entrepreneurs, and fostering an inclusive business environment will be critical for ensuring the long-term success and growth of women-owned businesses in Japan.

8.4 Management System in Japan

Managing global companies has many opportunities and challenges for the managers and the leadership of the company. Important support in facing all these challenges has been provided at cognitive level by management system models and at technological level by information technologies.

Toyota was the first company in Japan to start implementing Just-in-Time (JIT) management. JIT management is a crucial aspect of Japanese business culture and has significant implications for entrepreneurship in Japan. The basic idea of this management method, in contrast to the traditional one (raw materials bought by procurement departments, and then put into use as needed), consists in procuring raw materials from suppliers and putting them into use promptly without unnecessary stockpiling. In this way, stocks were minimized and constantly kept under control. The success of JIT in Toyota and in other companies in Japan consisted in the establishment of close relations between the manufacturing company and its suppliers. Namely, the basic characteristics of this management method consist of the following (Radović, 1993):

1. The company prefers to work with only one supplier. In order for a company's supplier to qualify, he must offer raw materials at the lowest prices and of the highest quality.
2. The supplier is ready to carry out daily delivery of raw materials and store them close to the manufacturing company, thereby reducing transportation costs and delivery time.
3. There is a close connection between the management of the company and the supplier, which can take the form of technical and financial cooperation.

This method was introduced not only in Japanese companies, but was also used in many countries around the world (USA, Europe, etc.).

Thus, in 14 months in the 1990s, the mentioned car factory "released" six new car models and achieved 43% of the total sales of cars in Japan (Radović, 1993). By the end of the 1990s, Toyota had sold more than a million cars in the US. Thus, in a short time, it changed its position on the international car market and rose from ninth to fourth place. This trend continued at the beginning of the new millennium. This Just-in-Time (JIT) system, as a key component of the Toyota Production System, has seen significant transformations in recent years. Namely, in recent years, many scholars have analyzed whether the JIT management system has transformed and how Japanese business organizations would remain globally competitive. Research has shown that a good management system has contributed to many Japanese manufacturing companies such as Toyota, Honda, and Canon still remaining competitive in the global market. The prosperity and survival of these companies was achieved thanks to their management, such as the implementation of a slightly modified (JIT) system and total quality management (TKM). It was simultaneously due to engineering and the ability to create a horizontal structure of connectivity in the entire communication network. It made it possible to continue the advantage of Japanese manufacturers, in addition to their technological advantages (Morita et al., 2001; Matsui and Sato, 2002). Some research has shown that JIT is still a powerful tool for Japanese manufacturers for global competition in 21st century (Matsui, 2007).

8.5 Conclusion

Entrepreneurship in Japan has been a topic of interest due to the country's unique economic and social landscape. First of all, cultural norms play an important role and influence on the entrepreneurial climate. For instance, there's a strong emphasis on job security and lifetime employment in large companies. In line with this, it can discourage entrepreneurial ventures. Also, entrepreneurs can create social change by offering new goods and services, breaking away from tradition, and reducing dependence on obsolete systems and technologies. However, this can be challenging in a society that values tradition and conformity. Namely, Japanese society traditionally respects authority and hierarchy. In the business world, this can manifest in a strong emphasis on leadership and decision-making structures within entrepreneurial ventures.

Secondly, the aging of the population is considered a big obstacle for the development of entrepreneurship in Japan. In response to these challenges, the Japanese government has taken measures such as increasing the mandatory retirement age from 55 to 65 and allowing workers to work after retirement (Eurasian Research Institute, 2019). These changes could potentially create a more diverse entrepreneurial landscape with more older individuals participating.

Third, the Japanese venture capital ecosystem has been growing, with increasing investment flowing into startups. This trend has been driven by both domestic and international investors seeking opportunities in Japan's tech sector. In this context, Japan has been increasingly focusing on tech startups, especially in areas such as AI, robotics, IoT, and fintech. The government has been supportive of these initiatives, promoting innovation through various programs and funding opportunities.

Fourth, several challenges linked to female entrepreneurship include cultural biases, limited access to funding and venture capital, difficulties balancing work and family responsibilities due to traditional gender roles, and a lack of female role models in entrepreneurship.

Finally, Japanese companies are known for their innovation and adoption of technology to enhance resilience. Namely, the development of contemporary technologies, especially the Internet on one side, and changes in management practice, communication, and the organization of work in companies on the other side, have led in the last years to changes with regards to knowledge type and acquisition methods (Radović et al., 2012). This implicates the use of new knowledge in the application of the best practical experience, as well as the experience of other organizations which are involved with the same or similar services.

References

Asian Development Outlook (September 2022). *Entrepreneurship in the Digital Age*. Asian Development Bank. Available at: Asian Development Outlook 2022 Update Background Papers | Asian Development Bank.

Chattergoon, B. (2018). Japan and Entrepreneurship: Culture Under the Microscope. *The Renaissance Economist.* Available at: Japan and Entrepreneurship: Culture Under the Microscope. | by Brad Chattergoon | The Renaissance Economist | Medium.

EduRank (2024). 4 Best Universities for Entrepreneurship in Japan. Available at: Japan's 4 best Entrepreneurship universities [2024 Rankings] (edurank.org)

Eurasian Research Institute (2019). The Consequences of Population Ageing in Japan. Available at: The Consequences of Population Ageing in Japan – ERI (eurasian-research.org).

GEM (2022). Entrepreneurial Behaviour and Attitudes. Available at: Entrepreneurship in Japan - GEM Global Entrepreneurship Monitor

GEM (2024). Global Report - 25 Years and Growing. Available at: GEM Global Entrepreneurship Monitor.

ItsJapanese Team (2024). 15+ Female Japanese Entrepreneurs & Their Stories. Available at: 15+ Female Japanese Entrepreneurs & Their Stories (itsjapanese.com)

J-Startup (n.d.). Next Growth for Japan's Startups, Next Innovation for the World. Available at: J-Startup

Matsui, Y. (2007). An Empirical Analysis of Just-in-Time Production in Japanese Manufacturing Companies. *International Journal of Production Economics*, Vol. 108, No. 1–2, July, pp. 153–164.

Matsui, Y., and Sato, O. (2002). An International Comparison Study on Benefits of Production Information Systems. *International Journal of Operation and Quantitative Management*, Vol. 8, No. 3, pp. 191–214.
Morita, M., Sakikabara, S., Matsui, Y., and Sato, O. (2001). Japanese Manufacturing Organization: Are They Still Competitive. In: Roger G. Schroeder and Barbara B. Flynn (Eds.), *High Performance Manufacturing: Global Perspectives*. New York: Wiley, pp. 199–232.
Radović, M. (1993). Strana iskustva u razvoju menadžmenta: Japan i Koreja. Privredni pregled.
Radović-Marković, M. et al. (2012). Freedom, Individuality and Women's Entrepreneurship Education. У: Catalin, M. & Druica, E. (eds.). Entrepreneurship education-a priority for the higher education institutions. Bologna: Medimond, pp. 2003–2008.
Radović Marković, M. (2022). Women Entrepreneurs' Resilience in Times Of Covid-19 And Afterwards. *Journal Entrepreneurship and Business Resilience*, Vol. 5, No. 2, pp. 25–30. Retrieved from https://jebr.fimek.edu.rs/index.php/jebr/article/view/79.
Radović Marković, M., Radulović, D., Đukanović, B., Kyaruzi S. I. (2021). *Flexibility and Adaptation – The New Post Covic Era*. Silver & Smith. ISBN978-1-80068-337-2.
Ruiu, G. and Breschi, M. (2019). The Effect of Aging on the Innovative Behavior of Entrepreneurs. *Journal of the Knowledge Economy*, Vol. 10, pp. 1784–1807.
SilverEco. (2016). Seniors make up a third of all Japanese entrepreneurs. Available at: Seniors make up a third of all Japanese entrepreneurs.
The Straits Times. (2022). Covid-19 pandemic has led to Japan's quiet work-from-home revolution. Available at: Covid-19 pandemic has led to Japan's quiet work-from-home revolution | The Straits Times.
WEF. (2023). More than 1 in 10 people in Japan are aged 80 or over. Here's how its ageing population is reshaping the country. Available at: Japan's ageing population: The implications for its economy | World Economic Forum
Wright, M (2022). Kaizen: The Japanese Management Style to Continuous Improvement. Available at: Kaizen: The Japanese Management Style to Continuous Improvement

A Book Conclusion

The book *Globalization and Entrepreneurship: Cases from China, Japan, and Bangladesh* presents a critical analysis of the impact of globalization on entrepreneurţship.

This book addresses the role of digital technologies that have become a new economic and social force, reshaping traditional business models, strategies, structures, and processes. In line with this, digital entrepreneurship, which focuses on creating new ventures and transforming existing businesses by developing new digital technologies or their novel usage, is seen as a critical pillar for economic growth, job creation, innovation, and poverty reduction of selected countries. To meet constantly changing conditions and demands, business must transcend boundaries to get what it needs regardless of where it exists—geographically, organizationally, and functionally. All these changings are shifting the traditional way of creating and doing business, determining the emergence of a new specific type of entrepreneurship.

This book explained that measuring the degree of globalization of a country involves assessing various economic, social, and political factors. The book has used some common indicators and methods to measure a country's level of globalization. Namely, the Global Index of Entrepreneurship is used to analyze the quality of entrepreneurship in the analyzed countries. We also used other indicators that showed us the specifics of development, as well as carefully selected literature.

Analyzing and comparing these three nations provides a multifaceted view of global dynamics, cultural richness, and economic interdependence. Each country contributes uniquely to the global mosaic, and understanding their interactions fosters a clearer view on our interconnected world.

DOI: 10.4324/9781003602378-13

Index

Note: Page numbers in **bold** and *italics* refer tables and figures, respectively.

www.ingramcontent.com/pod-product-compliance
Ingram Content Group UK Ltd.
Pitfield, Milton Keynes, MK11 3LW, UK
UKHW022109190926
475702UK00013B/1351
* 9 7 8 1 0 3 2 9 9 1 1 1 5 *